1,200 GREAT SALES TIPS

FOR
REAL
ESTATE
PROS

NATIONAL ASSOCIATION
OF REALTORS®
The Voice for Real Estate®

THE BUSINESS TOOL FOR REAL ESTATE PROFESSIONALS
REALTOR
MAGAZINE

1,200 GREAT SALES TIPS

FOR REAL ESTATE PROS

EDITED BY
CHRISTINA HOFFMANN SPIRA,
MANAGING EDITOR, *REALTOR*® *MAGAZINE*
WITH MARIWYN EVANS,
SENIOR EDITOR, *REALTOR*® *MAGAZINE*

BICENTENNIAL
1807
WILEY
2007
BICENTENNIAL

John Wiley & Sons, Inc.

Published by John Wiley & Sons, Inc., Hoboken, New Jersey.
Published simultaneously in Canada.

For general information on our other products and services or for technical support, please contact our Customer Care Department within the United States at (800) 762-2974, outside the United States at (317) 572-3993 or fax (317) 572-4002.

Wiley also publishes its books in a variety of electronic formats. Some content that appears in print may not be available in electronic books. For more information about Wiley products, visit our web site at www.wiley.com.

ISBN-13: 978-0-470-09689-5
ISBN-10: 0-470-09689-6

Printed in the United States of America.

10   9   8   7   6   5   4   3

Contents

Foreword

None of us gets more than 24 hours in a day. Yet the demands on our time and attention are endless. That truism was the impetus nearly five years ago for REALTOR® Magazine's first List Issue, an edition whose feature pages were devoted entirely to easy-to-scan tips for busy real estate professionals.

That first List Issue, in March 2003, was titled "How to Get It Done," and in my 15 years with the magazine, I'd never seen such a positive reaction to any issue. "'How to Get It Done' is beyond a shadow of a doubt the best publication ever written about real estate!" wrote one reader. Another said, " 'How to Get It Done' was worth two dozen seminars." With that kind of response—and so many more lists in our heads—we decided to make the List Issue an annual event. The thank-you letters kept coming after each issue, so early this year we decided it was time for a book.

This is REALTOR® Magazine's second book published using popular content from the magazine. Our first book, *Broker to Broker: Management Lessons from America's Most Successful Real Estate Companies* (John Wiley & Sons, 2005), edited by Senior Editor Robert Freedman, was devoted to brokerage managers. For this book, Managing Editor Christina Hoffmann Spira has put the focus on sales professionals—combing through four years worth of lists to find the best tips we could bring you on prospecting, marketing, business planning, professional development, and more. Just as important, you'll find clear, up-to-date guidance on how to keep your sales efforts legal. For those of you who want to go beyond what's here, find additional resources, including related articles, books, eBooks, and web sites, related to each chapter at the end of this book.

With *Broker to Broker* and now *1,200 Great Sales Tips for Real Estate Pros*, we're happy to extend the magazine's mission of being "The Business Tool for Real Estate Professionals." But we have an underlying mission, too, one that we share with all magazines: a desire to facilitate an ongoing conversation with and among readers. That's the value we hope to bring you with this book and with our annual List Issue going forward. I hope you'll take a few moments to write to us and share your thoughts on the book and your ideas for future lists. Thank you.

Stacey Moncrieff
REALTOR® Magazine Editor
November 2006

You can write to the magazine at
REALTOR® Magazine
NATIONAL ASSOCIATION OF REALTORS®
430 N. Michigan Ave.
Chicago, IL 60611-4087

Or send an e-mail to
narpubs@realtors.org

Introduction

YOUR SEMINAR-TO-GO

Learning every day energizes you and gives you a highly competitive edge.

> —Carol McManus, vice president of learning development and infrastructure for Realogy Corporation, formerly Cendant

There's no debate among the best and the brightest: Ongoing education isn't an option; it's a necessity. It's a matter of get educated or get eliminated. The only way to survive and succeed in today's real estate business is to constantly learn more about the business and the people you serve. This need for a daily knowledge infusion is the reason REALTOR® Magazine decided to publish this book of ideas.

"Smart salespeople get ongoing training because they take responsibility for their own success," says Floyd Wickman, a real estate speaker and trainer based in South Easton, Massachusetts.

Wickman believes industry changes have made the way you did business just a few years ago utterly obsolete. "Buyers and sellers are more educated, but not always the right way. The old idea of simply advising clients of the best decisions doesn't work because they believe they know so much. Only highly skilled practitioners have the credibility to convince buyers and sellers to make the best decisions in a changing market."

Educating yourself was important during the real estate boom when it was easy to overlook a critical detail as you tried to keep atop the pounding pace of deals. But education is even more vital in today's changing industry and market. You need to dust off and touch up those rusty property marketing skills. You have to use successful strategies from top performers and trainers to fuel your own creativity and jump-start your motivation.

Practitioners today need "skills for a changing market," says Carol McManus, vice president of learning development and infrastructure for the Realogy Corporation, formerly Cendant. Increased inventory and longer on-market times mean "a stronger relationship with buyers is just as important."

Howard Chung, vice president of Washington Residential Operations for John L. Scott Real Estate in Bellevue, Washington, points up other important changes. "The way we're paid is being challenged, so it's very important for practitioners to understand their value proposition," he says. "There's also a generational shift. For example, more and more young people are buying their first condo or home, so you have to make sure you're in tune with that generation."

So, if everyone agrees that ongoing training is critical, what's the problem?

"Our CEO likes to say that sometimes [real estate practitioners] play in the same sandbox too often," says Chung. "We don't try things outside our sandbox, which means we end up doing the same things over and over."

Indeed, being successful in real estate comes from letting sand from other practitioners' sandbox spill into yours, Chung says.

"When you meet with other salespeople, they share ideas that may be new to you."

In addition, "Our unplanned commitments interfere with getting to training sessions," says McManus. After all, who's going to say, "I'm sorry, I have to go to a seminar," to a buyer who's ready to make an offer on a house? This chronic time crunch is a big reason companies have expanded their online and video training and the NATIONAL ASSOCIATION OF REALTORS® (NAR) has launched its eBooks program (http://ebooks.realtor.org), which allows NAR members to check out books digitally from the association's library. (And the reason that quick-read, portable education tools such as this book are so valuable to busy practitioners.)

Complacency is another factor in skipped training, says Dianna Kokoszka, vice president of Mega Achievement Productivity Systems for Keller Williams Realty in Austin, Texas. "When you're new, you want training and know how valuable it is," she says. "As you become seasoned, you think, 'I'm selling 20 to 30 houses a year. I'm doing well. I don't need training.' If we think we're great, we're never going to get better."

Some experienced salespeople also think that once they've been through a course, they don't need to go back, says Kokoszka.

Wrong! "Each time you go to a class or reread an article, you pick up something new," she says. "As you advance, you hear more things."

Chung says training also gets short shrift because many courses seem "mundane and administrative. People aren't interested in [plain] information," he says. "They're interested in information that includes a healthy dose of inspiration, which can change behavior."

Busy salespeople also need quick answers that address the challenge of the moment, says Chung. "They're saying, 'Give me scripts, dialogue, and strategies I can use to articulate that I'm worth my commission,'" he says. "At a time when the market isn't as good as it was over the past six years, they're also asking, 'How do I handle objections? How do I negotiate? How do I pitch myself?'"

It's just these sorts of strategies and scripts you'll find in *1,200 Great Sales Tips for Real Estate Pros*. Packed with the best ideas from the best trainers, brokers, and salespeople in the business, this weeklong seminar between two covers will prepare you for the future and pave your way to a more successful business.

Convinced? Then what are you waiting for? Slip this book into your briefcase, keep a copy in your desk, or throw one on the front seat of your car. Next time you're stuck for a selling strategy, need a little motivational pick-me-up, or have five spare minutes to expand your skills, just flip it open and learn away. The quick lists and tips make it easy to find and absorb knowledge fast. Choose any page, and you'll take away a new idea to grow your business and build your life.

As the father of total quality management, W. Edwards Deming, said, "Learning is not compulsory . . . neither is survival."

—REALTOR® Magazine editors

Chapter 1

PROSPECTING

Striking Real Estate Gold

When gold fever struck California in 1849, prospectors armed with pickaxes, shovels, and pans followed their maps to where the gold was.

Prospecting for real estate listings, potential buyers, and referrals also requires a plan and the right tools. You need to zero in on your sphere of influence—those who know and respect you and are most likely to hire or refer you to others—rather than depend on random efforts like standing in a shopping mall at a kiosk and waiting for someone to walk by, says Dave Beson, a broker and head of Dave Beson Seminars in Minneapolis.

Once you narrow your list of prospects, develop a consistent program of "touches." Regularly e-mail, telephone, snail mail, and meet face-to-face with prospects. When you get their attention, deliver a message that's appropriate and that touches each person emotionally, Beson says. If they've just bought a house, send a welcome postcard with a list of favorite area shops.

But don't stop there. Stay in contact and feed prospects the information they most want: what comparable area houses are selling for, says Kenneth W. Edwards, founder of Professional Associates in Corvallis, Oregon, and author of *Your Successful Real Estate Career* (AMACOM, 2003). If you keep your name out front, prospects are likely to remember you when they get ready to sell.

Also, remember never to rely on one approach. Develop a multilayered campaign. If you're worried about becoming a pest, don't. "It's better prospects see you as the one who followed up seven times. They'll know you're on their side," Beson says.

If by chance they find your style irksome, you'll learn an invaluable lesson in prospecting—and life. You can't be successful all the time, but you can develop resiliency. Get back on your feet; start anew. Next time you'll prospect better. Here are more lessons to start you on your way.

🏠 *12 Prospecting Tips*

Build a wide sphere of influence through regular prospecting. There's no time like the present to improve your skills with these handy tips.

1. *Add a memo field to your contacts database* to store pertinent, personal information about prospects. For example, planned retirement in two years, children going to college, or a big promotion.

2. *Conduct a phone survey.* Choose a topic that's likely to be of interest to your prospects—the impact of recent school reform or how the current economy is affecting the neighborhood. Then offer to e-mail the survey results. Voilà, you have an instant e-mail marketing list. (Before you pick up the phone, know your state's antisolicitation laws. Surveys

aren't prohibited under the national do not call laws, but you can't talk about or sell your services to people over the phone at the same time. Keep the call strictly to research.)

3. *Motivate yourself* to prospect by making a deal to pay a fellow associate $10 a day for every day you don't cold-call for one hour.

4. *Analyze the language* used in FSBO ads and adapt your marketing presentation to fit the style of each prospect.

5. *Smile when you pick up the phone.* Experts say the simple act of smiling subtly alters your voice and manner and makes you more approachable.

6. *When you're setting up a listing appointment,* be sure you're talking to the decision maker.

7. *When you call to introduce yourself,* ask if the prospect is busy. If so, ask for a convenient time to call again.

8. *Hand-address your letters.* It increases the likelihood that they'll be opened. Mailing too many letters to hand-address? Choose a computer typeface that looks like handwriting.

9. *Contact your best prospects first* in case you run out of time.

10. *Build your e-mail list* by sponsoring an occasional online contest. Tell interested prospects they must enter via e-mail and will be notified the same way. Offer a good prize—a television or dinner for two at a hot restaurant. For each contest offer a different kind of prize. Sooner or later, you'll motivate most people to participate. (Contests are regulated in every state. Check with your state attorney general's office for regulations.)

11. *Ask prospects for a five-minute appointment* in return for your tips on how to increase their home's value.

12. *While at a fast-food drive-through*, pay for coffee for the car behind you. Ask the clerk to hand your business card to the driver. You might get a call or e-mail with thanks.

Sources: Dave Beson, Dave Beson Seminars, Minneapolis; Denise Brophy, RE/MAX Realty Specialists, St. John's, Newfoundland; Chip Franks, The Real Estate Marketplace, Killeen, Texas; Raymond C. Harlan and Walter M. Woolfson, *Telemarketing That Works* (McGraw-Hill, 1991); Joe Meyer, Joe Meyer Presentations, Lake Grove, N.Y.; Jack O'Connor, Prestige Real Estate Group, Englewood, Colo.

🏠 6 Creative Prospecting Events

If you host it, they will come. Here are some great ways to draw prospects out of the woodwork and into your database.

1. Ask if you can take instant photos of Halloween trick-or-treaters when they come to your door. Slip the photos into jackets printed with your name and telephone number and give them to the parents.

2. Create a competition to award a $500 or $1,000 college scholarship to a high school senior in your community. Present the check at a ceremony for the winner's family and friends.

3. Buy a block of tickets to a concert or play and hold a drawing in your office. Call past customers and ask whether they'd like their names to be in the hopper.

4. Sponsor a home repair demonstration or lecture at a local hardware or home improvement store.

5. During the summer, rent an ice cream truck and give away free frozen goodies in targeted neighborhoods. Use a postcard mailing to notify residents ahead of time.

6. Organize a group to go caroling in your market area. You can leave behind your company's holiday card at each home you visit.

Source: REALTOR® Magazine Online's (REALTOR.org/realtormag) Personal Marketing section.

🏠 *Powerful Prelisting*

Prelisting packets may be the first and most important impression you make on sellers. The goal of the kit, according to David Knox of Minneapolis-based David Knox Productions Inc., is to establish credibility, not to sell. Focus on materials that focus on you.

Here's what your prelisting packet should include:

- *Cover letter.* Remind prospects when you'll arrive and how to contact you.

- *Outline of your skills.* Be sure your brochures and resume describe your qualifications, experience, and designations.

- *Personal marketing brochure.* Reuse the same brochure you mail for personal marketing efforts. Be sure your materials explain your selling philosophy, marketing approach, and commitment to top-notch service.

- *Brief bios of your team members.* Highlight each person's experience and the functions they'll perform for the seller. Include a friendly, informal picture of team members so that the sellers feel they know them.

- *Testimonials from past clients.* It's always more effective if someone else says something positive about you than saying it yourself, says real estate marketer and author Danielle Kennedy of Danielle Kennedy Productions in Pacific Palisades, California.

- *A few press clippings* about you and one or two articles you have written. Nothing creates credibility better than the endorsement of a third party.

- *A property disclosure* for the sellers to complete. Ask questions on the age of the house, appliances, roof, and furnace. Ask them to note any environmental issues, give costs of annual property taxes and assessment, and point out any special features connected with the house.

Meet the Buyers

Helping people buy their first home is a great start to a long-term relationship. Here are some tips on how to meet first-time buyers.

At Weddings

I've found friends of the bride and groom start thinking about their own long-term goals as soon as the couple rides off into the sunset. Young people want direction from someone who is knowledgeable and who cares.

—*Ann Marie McManus, Meybohm Realty Inc.,
Augusta, Georgia*

Through Tax Preparers

Every renter who files a tax return and doesn't have property ownership benefits is a candidate.

> —*Bob Taylor, Weir, Manuel, Snyder & Ranke LLC,*
> *REALTORS®, Birmingham, Michigan*

At Bridal Shows

We set up information booths to promote the benefits of home ownership and to show attendees how easy it is to buy.

> —*James Raysbrook, Coldwell Banker Bain Associates,*
> *Bellevue, Washington*

At Apartment Complexes

These are often the best places to prospect for new buyers. Door hangers, flyers, postcards, and info sessions are excellent ways to reach out to the residents.

> —*Kristin Carvalho, ROI Group, Keller Williams Integrity*
> *First Realty, Mesa, Arizona*

During a Workout

We meet more first-time buyers at the gym than at any other place. By working with the health club's general manager or salespeople to design a new-member packet with information on me and other area businesses, my team and I are able to provide an added benefit to gym members and acquire leads.

> —*Adam Mullen, Realty Executives Greater Atlanta,*
> *Alpharetta, Georgia*

At PTA and School Functions

Teachers are excellent candidates for new homes. In my market area, there's a grant program designed specifically for teachers, and I always mention this while working within the PTA.

—Shontell Rucker, Rekcur Properties, Houston

23 *Steps for Generating More Leads*

The salesperson who converts the most leads wins. Here are tips for capturing five of the most steady sources of business.

Expireds

1. Block off time regularly to research the Multiple Listing Service (MLS) for listings that are about to expire.

2. After a listing expires, call, send a letter, or make a personal visit to the seller.

3. Instead of asking for the business, be prepared with a list of services you offer, such as a free value analysis or a free prelisting consultation. If the sellers aren't home, let them know they can visit your web site for a list of your services.

4. Be more persistent than the competition. Start with two phone calls, then send a letter, then try a personal visit during a three-week time period. If there's still no activity, move on to the next lead.

Foreclosures

5. Identify delinquents, either through a subscription service that tracks default filings or by following notices in your

local newspaper. Solve the homeowner's problem with a sale and you've solved the bank's problem, too.

6. People who bought at the top of a real estate market cycle might find themselves with a loan-over-value problem. Contact these people and, if they're interested in selling, work with them and the lender on a short sale. Again, you're solving a problem for both the seller and the bank.

7. Assemble a team of handymen, painters, landscapers, carpet people, board-up companies, and other service providers so that you can offer one-stop service.

8. Promote your workout and bank-owned property services to lenders in your area, as well as Fannie Mae and Freddie Mac.

FSBOs

9. Block off time every week to research FSBOs. Leads can come from family and friends, local newspapers, and FSBO web sites.

10. Team up with a lender who can call FSBOs and offer services such as buyer preapproval. The lender can offer to refer them to a reliable salesperson (you) for a chance to handle the loan for the buyer.

11. Have third-party endorsements from former FSBOs, success stories, marketing ideas, and other materials ready to share with those who haven't been able to successfully sell on their own.

12. If your lender partner handles a loan on a FSBO sale, ask for a referral to help the FSBOs find their new home.

Online Inquiries

13. Add all leads to a database, and contact each lead three times over the course of two or three weeks. No response? Discard it or move it into a lower priority group for later follow-up.

14. Implement a database mailing plan so that everyone in your database receives a mailing from you each quarter. Since these communications most likely will be through e-mail, keep each lead in your database until told by the recipient to delete it.

15. Match seller "haves" with buyer "wants." That is, use your knowledge about what online prospects want to win listings ("I know of three potential buyers who are looking for homes in your neighborhood"). And use your knowledge of the inventory to win buyer clients ("I know of or have several listings that meet your criteria").

16. Test offers on your web site to see how effectively they generate incoming leads. Keep popular offers, such as determining the price of a recent neighborhood sale, and expand your offer list over time.

17. Test strategies for maximizing site visits. Two popular methods are paying search engines for prominent placement and increasing the number of reciprocal links with other web sites.

Open Houses

18. Arrange an open house caravan for eight listings—including possibly the listings of colleagues—that are within five minutes' drive time and within 20 percent of a target value.

19. Work with your colleagues and the sellers to arrange a day in which you'll host a 15-minute open house for each listing, with time between each for driving.

20. Place an ad in the newspaper promoting the eight open houses, yourself, the other salespeople whose listings you're showing, and your lender.

21. Send invitations, with a schedule and maps of the route, to neighbors of all the sellers. Aim to send at least 50 invitations. Serve refreshments at all the houses, and have a drawing for a prize, such as a lottery ticket or gift certificate to a local restaurant, at the last home.

22. Have the lender go with you to prequalify prospects.

23. Make the last two stops secret homes, such as FSBO properties. Get permission first.

Source: Walter S. Sanford, Sanford Systems and Strategies (www.waltersanford .com), Kankakee, Ill.

🏠 *15 Innovative Ideas for Building Referrals*

Past customers aren't the only ones who can send business your way. Here are ideas for increasing referrals.

1. I buy a table at a charity event, school fundraiser, or chamber of commerce mixer. I invite some clients and encourage them each to invite a friend. Now I'm not a broker but the guy who invited them to dinner. At some point during the conversation I'm usually introduced as somebody's broker and it's almost by osmosis that I become their friend's broker, too. *—Daniel Webster Johnson, RE/MAX Properties of the Summit, Breckenridge, Colorado*

2. I've made it a point to get to know the people who answer the phones and handle administrative work for rental apartments, property management companies, and condo offices. They know when leases are coming up, and tenants and owners alike always seem to let them know well ahead of time what their buying or selling intentions are. —*Brad Kintz, Long & Foster Real Estate, Alexandria, Virginia*

3. I'm a full-time working mother and find many of my referrals are generated through local activities that involve my child—music classes, my babysitter, playgroups. People with young children can see that I understand the needs of young families who want to stay in the same area but need more space. —*Nancy Tassone, JDL Brokerage Co., Chicago*

4. One way to generate more referrals is to join a business referral group such as Business Network International (www.bni.com). This will provide you with a "board of directors" for your business and a steady stream of referrals. —*Mary Zentz, RE/MAX Suburban, Arlington Heights, Illinois*

5. I set up an e-mail list of my high school and college classmates, as well as other alumni. I let them know that I'm in real estate and explain how I can help them, their family and friends, and their co-workers. If they're outside of my service area, I offer to help them identify qualified real estate professionals in their area. —*Jamal Smith, Keller Williams Real Estate, Blue Bell, Pennsylvania*

6. Develop a memorable, 60-second oral description of what you do—"I help people find the home they've always dreamed of"—and use it to describe your work to new acquaintances. —*Ivan Misner, Business Network International, Upland, California*

7. Attach a Post-it note reading "FYI" and your initials to your newsletter or to an article of interest, and give it to clients. The note helps attract people's attention and makes the correspondence seem more personal.

8. Give past clients vouchers for a free 30-minute consultation with you that they can pass on to friends and family. —*Patrick Seroka, "Keeping the Customer for Life,"* Mortgage Banking, *February 2000*

9. Offer real estate advice via your local paper or radio station to establish your presence in the community.

10. Choose a unique gift to send to past clients and referral sources each year—a special cake, a Halloween pumpkin, a spring flower arrangement—then repeat the same gift for several years. People will come to expect the gift and associate it with you in their minds.

11. Donate an annual amount to a local charity in the name of all your past clients and notify them of your gift.

12. Offer to work with a local insurance agent to help homeowners re-evaluate the adequacy of their property insurance.

13. Work with a local college to present an annual economic forecast breakfast. Speak about the real estate market and ask one or two local business leaders to share their ideas on the future.

14. Take up a new interest. It will expose you to a different group of people that you might not otherwise encounter. If you've always been a sports fan, try a reading group. Or take group golf lessons if your idea of exercise is walking from the car to the mall.

15. Ask. Let people know that you welcome referral business.

Compiled by REALTOR® Magazine's editorial staff.

7 More No-Fail Referral Ideas

Here's some welcome news: 44 percent of buyers choose a sales-person based on the recommendation of a friend, neighbor, or family member. Try these to increase referrals:

1. *Give past clients two coupon books*, each offering a free consultation with you about the real estate topic of their choice—adding curb appeal, sprucing up the interior before a sale, learning about the top remodeling projects in your market. Ask them to pass one of the books to a family member, friend, or colleague.

2. *Raise your media profile.* Write a regular column for an area newspaper, host a call-in radio show about hot real estate topics, or teach a course at a local college.

3. *Host an hors d'oeuvres-and-drinks appreciation night at a favorite restaurant.* Ask your contacts to invite a friend, colleague, or relative. Give away goodie bags imprinted with your name, company, phone, e-mail, and web address.

4. *Take up a new hobby or enroll in a course.* It's a great way to meet future clients. Possibilities: a book club, group dancing lessons, or a computer or cooking class.

5. *Sponsor a children's sports team.* Don't just pay for jerseys imprinted with your company name. Help coach so that you get to know the parents and the kids.

6. *Network with allied professionals.* Mortgage lenders, builders, developers, architects, interior decorators, and kitchen and bath designers all are good referral sources—and they'll appreciate referrals from you, too.

7. *Host a housewarming party* for recent buyers at which you cook, serve, and clean up.

Sources: 2005 NATIONAL ASSOCIATION OF REALTORS® *Profile of Home Buyers and Sellers* and REALTOR® Magazine Online (REALTOR.org/realtormag).

8-Step Personal Marketing Plan

A personal marketing plan is a written document that describes the business goals you expect to accomplish and strategies and activities you will do to reach those goals. A marketing plan should include:

1. *Objectives and Goals.* First, develop a big-picture vision for your business—become the top producer in your area, retire in 10 years. Then quantify that vision with measurable goals. Measurable goals might include:

   ■ Obtaining 50 listings in the next year.

   ■ Achieving a 60 percent name recognition in your target market area.

   ■ Receiving referrals from 75 percent of your past customers or sphere of influence.

   ■ Securing a 20 percent share of the market in your target area.

   TIP Determine your market share by dividing the number of sales you made by the total number of annual sales in your target market. The result is your percentage share of the market.

2. *Audience.* Select one or two groups to target with your marketing efforts. Analyze the characteristics of your best

prospects; other groups with similar qualities may be the best place to start. Characteristics might be:

- Income brackets.

- Age groups.

- Geographic areas.

- Ethnic or cultural groups.

- Levels of education or certain professions.

- Lifestyles, such as golfers buying second homes.

3. *Differentiation.* What makes you unique? Setting yourself apart from other salespeople is essential in a crowded marketplace. Remember: Customers choose products and services based on the benefits they deliver. Consider your own strengths and weaknesses, and focus on the qualities and skills that make you special to potential customers. Possible points of differentiation are:

- Education—law degree, CPA, and so on. (Benefit: knowledge of legal and financial issues can make the transaction process easier.)

- Residency in the neighborhood you represent. (Benefit: knowledge of available services, activities, and interests of prospective neighbors).

- A leadership role in a community or professional group. (Benefit: first access to new ideas in the industry and sources of solutions to problems via networking).

- A natural affinity for a certain group—seniors, for example. (Benefit: a special understanding of the needs and desires of that group).

4. *Message.* Select a message and sales approach that will grab the attention of the people you want to target. The message should highlight what makes you different from your com-

petitors and have an emotional appeal to your target market. An emotional appeal speaks to what people want—security, a sense of family, financial security—and focuses on their needs and desires.

5. *Media*. Select two or three media to convey your message and allow for cross marketing among several different sources. Media choices include print advertising, brochures, a web page, in-person marketing, community involvement, and so on.

6. *Action Plan and Schedule*. Basically an action plan is a to-do list for a set period that lists every activity you need to do to market yourself and your services. Consistency is a key component to successful marketing. Advertising experts say that people must hear a message 11 times before they remember it. Make a commitment to use one marketing approach for at least six months, and budget accordingly.

7. *Budget*. The most challenging aspect of creating a personal marketing budget is estimating costs. Rather than guessing, call your suppliers and service providers, tell them you're preparing a budget, and ask them to provide estimates of the price you can expect to pay for each item. Ask your suppliers about quantity discounts and other ways to cut costs. The total cost for your personal marketing effort will depend on the size of your target market and the media you choose.

8. *Measurement*. Are you achieving the goals you set forth in your plan? You will never know if you don't measure. Always ask callers where they heard about you, and keep track of their responses. Use small letter codes in direct mail to identify each piece for easier tracking. Analyze the results of your measurement and use your conclusions to update, revise, and improve your personal marketing

campaign. Don't continue to spend money on something that isn't working.

TIP   One way to measure success is by the cost per contact. If you mailed out 500 brochures at a cost of $2,500 and received 10 inquiry calls, your cost per contact is $250.

Compiled by REALTOR® Magazine's editorial staff.

6 Ways to Get Involved in Your Community

Community service gives you the chance to network with other real estate professionals, build relationships in your local business community, make contact with potential clients, and find an avenue to express yourself outside of work. Follow these simple tips to get more involved.

1. Find an area of service that you think is fulfilling. You may be interested in working with the elderly, the poor, or children. Look for ways to work with issues that have personal meaning for you or someone you care about.

2. Attend events held by volunteer organizations to see if you would fit into the organizations' opportunities and the people they serve.

3. Determine the realistic amount of time you have to offer. Don't worry if you start out small—it's more important to be consistent and live up to your promised commitment.

4. Volunteer for special one-time events, such as outings for seniors, hospital parties, or other projects where extra hands are needed. It will give you a chance to see what the organization is like.

5. Investigate a charity you want to work with to make sure that it spends a small percentage of its donations on overhead.

6. Look in your own backyard. Most state and many local REALTOR® associations have organized volunteer efforts that would welcome your support.

Adapted from REALTOR® Magazine Online's (REALTOR.org/realtormag) Good Neighbors and For Rookies sections.

6 Ways to Build Trust

Once you lose someone's trust, it's almost impossible to regain it. Here are six tips on how to get started down the right path.

1. *Be trustworthy.* When you give your word, keep it. If you can't deliver on a promise, acknowledge it as soon as possible and develop a secondary plan.

2. *Tell the truth.* Once you've been caught in a lie, you've lost your credibility. If there's something you can't say, say so and tell the other person why.

3. *Be honest with yourself, first.* If something troubles you, it's likely to trouble others as well.

4. *Think twice.* Before you say or do something, ask yourself how it would look to an outside observer.

5. *Don't be a hypocrite.* There's no faster way to lose someone's trust than if your actions contradict your words.

6. *Do good things early and often.* If you make a habit of rewarding and praising people, they're less likely to question your motivation.

Source: Stever Robbins, The Stever Robbins Company (www.steverrobbins.com), Cambridge, Mass.

🏠 *Phone-Free Prospecting*

Feel sidetracked by the no-call rules? The rules limit your prospecting ability only if you let them. You can achieve success in prospecting using e-mail or snail mail. Here's how to initiate personal contact without a telephone:

- Send regular e-mail messages or letters to friends, family, neighbors, and past customers reminding them that you're actively engaged in the real estate business. *Note:* With e-mail, be sure your messages follow the guidelines of the federal CAN-SPAM Act.

- In the letters, always include some information of value—how to protest property tax increases, what spring maintenance your contacts should consider on their house, recent sales trends. This'll let people know you're looking out for their interests, not just your livelihood.

- Always end the letter with a friendly request for referrals. To be referral-worthy, do what you say you'll do when you say you will. If someone responds to a letter on spring maintenance by asking you to recommend good window washers, call back right away to tell the person you're on it, and then have an answer within 24 hours.

Source: Dirk Zeller, Real Estate Champions, Bend, Ore., and author of *Your 1st Year in Real Estate: Making the Transition from Total Novice to Successful Professional* (Three Rivers Press, 2001).

🏠 *Abide by No-Call Rules: 9 Tips*

Don't throw away prospects' telephone numbers—but use them more judiciously and creatively as you hunt for business under the glare of the National Do Not Call Registry.

1. *Know whom not to call.* Register on the Federal Trade Commission's (FTC's) web site, https://telemarketing.donotcall.gov, to access the database of consumers who've elected not to receive telemarketing calls. Consumers can register both residential and cell phone numbers. You can receive names for up to five area codes free of charge. Beyond that, you pay an annual fee per area code. Update your list every month.

2. *Continue to call those who aren't on the list, as well as close contacts who are.* The rules make an exception for warm calls to friends and acquaintances who wouldn't be surprised or offended to receive your call.

3. *When you call, include a discreet real estate pitch.* Say something to the effect of "Hi, Barbara, this is Pete Potter. I'm updating the database for my e-newsletter and wondered if you'd share your e-mail address so I could send a copy to you. The newsletter has a community events feature I think you'll like." Toward the end of the conversation, drop in some real estate tidbit.

4. *Send letters to prospects whose names are on the list.* Tell them that you respect their wishes and are available to help if they're buying or selling.

5. *Stay in contact with buyers and sellers you've recently worked with.* An exception under the FTC rules allows you to call

customers with whom you had a business relationship in the past 18 months. Be tactful when you touch base. Ask how they're doing and inquire whether there's anything you can do for them. Many real estate professionals fail to follow up, fearing they'll hear complaints. Consider complaints an opportunity to solve a problem.

6. *Follow up with those who've recently called you to inquire about a listing.* They fall into another exception category. You can call them for up to three months after their query. People who've signed in at an open house or called a property information hotline also can be called within the same time frame.

7. *Call FSBOs with an advertised telephone number*, since they, too, have invited inquiries, but only if you have a buyer who's interested in their property.

8. *Contact FSBOs and expireds by door knocking.* Agree to a short listing period if they're willing to price their property to sell. Always thank them for their time.

9. *Follow up a phone call or visit with a handwritten note on nice stationery.* Your note won't be confused with junk mail and keeps your name in buyers' minds.

Sources: Pam Beard, BrokerSouth GMAC Real Estate, Vicksburg, Miss.; Michigan Association of REALTORS®; REALTOR® Magazine Online (REALTOR.org/realtor mag); John Stewart and Robbie Hunt, F. C. Tucker Company Inc., Indianapolis; Allen Tappe, author, *Selling Real Estate on Purpose* (The Institute for Purposed Performance, 2002) and president of The Tappe Group, Arlington, Texas.

 ## Bring FSBOs to You

Want to convert more FSBOs? Put together a service package that includes information they'll need to sell on their own. When they decide to hire a listing agent, they'll call you. Here are several documents to include in the packet:

- Net sheet for calculating what they'll realize in the transaction.
- List of inspections buyers often request or require (home, termite, radon).
- Property condition disclosure form, with an explanation of your state's disclosure requirements.
- Lead-based paint disclosure brochure from HUD.
- Tips for getting a home ready for sale.
- Tips for conducting an open house.
- Explanation of how to qualify buyers.

Source: REALTOR® Magazine Online's (REALTOR.org/realtormag) "Converting FSBOs" Prepackaged Sales Meeting.

5 Favorite FSBO Flips

Be prepared with these field-tested responses, and you won't let a FSBO objection keep you from getting a listing.

1. *If the FSBO says*: "I'm sure I'll get a buyer in no time. I've had the house on the market only one week, and I've already had three people come to see it."

   Counter with: "It's great that you've had so much interest, but how many of those people have come back a second time? One of the problems with showing a house is that you get a lot of browsers who just like to see other people's homes."

2. *If the FSBO says*: "I can't afford to pay a real estate commission. I need every cent I can get from the sale to put toward my new house."

   Counter with: "I know it's important to have the biggest down payment possible. But a NATIONAL ASSOCIATION OF REALTORS® survey, the *2005 Profile of Home Buyers and Sellers*, found that the median selling price of a FSBO home was $198,200 compared with $230,000 for agent-assisted home sales. So even with my commission, you'll probably come out ahead. Other statistics from the survey that also might aid your argument: 39 percent of buyers said the salesperson helped shorten the home search; 36 percent said the salespeople helped negotiate better contract terms; and 29 percent said the salesperson helped negotiate a better sales price.

3. *If the FSBO says*: "What do I need you for? I can put up a sign in my yard."

   Counter with: "It's true that your sign will attract buyers, but many of them won't be able to afford your home. When I get a call from a house sign, I can prequalify buyers. In addition, I won't just put up a sign. I'll actively market your listing, through the MLS and other means, to brokers who are already working with qualified buyers."

4. *If the FSBO says*: "If I list my property, it will be with my friend who's in real estate."

   Counter with: "It's great to be loyal to your friends. But can you afford to list your property with a friend for 60 or 90 days and take the chance that it won't sell? If you're planning to buy another home, that's a big gamble. Our company sells homes in your area fast. (Provide the number of days on market.) Also, I've found that when working with friends, it's hard to fire them if they don't perform."

5. *If the FSBO says*: "I can do this myself."

   Counter with: "Of course, you're smart enough to do what has to be done. But why spend all the time figuring out something you may not do more than a few times in your life? Let someone who has experience do the work for you."

   If you decide to try to sell on your own, I'll be glad to give you a list of all the forms you'll need. (Quantify the number of forms to demonstrate the sheer volume of paperwork involved in selling a home.)

Source: REALTOR® Magazine Online's (REALTOR.org/realtormag) "Converting FSBOs" Prepackaged Sales Meeting.

When a Friend Goes FSBO

Problem: You're driving through your market area when you notice a past client—someone you've maintained a friendly relationship with during the past three years—has a FSBO sign in front of his house. What do you do?

Solution: Rather than immediately calling to ask him why he isn't planning to work with you, do a little research. Dig out the old files and examine the last transaction you had with the client. There might be clues as to why he's trying the FSBO route. Ask yourself these questions:

1. Were there significant problems with the transaction that the client might be blaming on you?

2. Did you follow up as well as you should have during and after the transaction?

3. Did the transaction go quickly? Perhaps your friend thinks you didn't do much work or need much skill on the last transaction and, therefore, he could do it himself and save money.

Once you've evaluated the file, get in touch with him as soon as possible. Keep a friendly tone. Your goal is to discover why he's going FSBO without expressing shock, anger, or disappointment.

One possibility might be that his family is in financial straits and he's embarrassed. Ask him how things are going with the marketing and let him open up. He'll know your underlying desire is to snag the listing. But also let him know what's more important to you: helping him through this difficult time in any way you can—whether that means giving him advice on his marketing, sending buyers his way, or helping him understand the ramifications of a short sale.

If your friend doesn't have an explanation, then you can ask, without bitterness: "I wonder if you could tell me why you didn't consider calling me. I work hard to maintain good relationships with past clients, and many do come back to me when they're ready to move again." Let him know you're a little confused because you felt that you gave his family great service. If he says the last transaction seemed easy, smile and thank him. Tell him you take great pride in making every transaction appear easier than it really is. Then review all the steps and tasks you take in a transaction to make it go as smoothly as possible. Most people probably aren't aware of everything you do.

If there was a problem with the last transaction, discuss it openly. Explain that had the sale been handled by another practitioner or attempted as a FSBO, it might not have gone through at all.

If the conversation doesn't get you closer to winning the list-ing, then treat your friend professionally as you would any other FSBO. Follow up frequently. Offer friendly assistance. He'll soon see how difficult it can be to sell on his own. By then, you'll have regained his trust and, with luck, his listing.

Source: Joe Meyer, Joe Meyer Presentations Inc. (www.joemeyer.com), Lake Grove, N.Y.

Get Better Results from Your Direct Mail

Studies show that an effective direct mail campaign should draw a 0.5 percent to 1 percent response. These tips will help you and your associates get the results you want.

1. *A bold headline.* Include a single, central message on the en-velope or the front of the postcard. Example: "The Hansen Team Sells More Real Estate." The headline should fill at least 15 percent of the front of the mailer.

2. *A graphic that reinforces the central message.* The graphic should be easy to understand. Example: a home with a SOLD sign clearly visible.

3. *Color that pops.* When you look at a mock-up of the card, do you see the headline first? Make the headline and other text stand out by using a color that contrasts with the back-ground color.

4. *Subheads that lead into text.* If your mailer includes more than 100 words of text, you need to entice people to read the copy. A subhead gives people a place to start.

5. *Benefits, benefits, benefits.* One of the biggest errors people make in advertising is stating features rather than benefits.

Never assume recipients know what benefit can be derived from a lower interest rate on their mortgage, for example. Let them know how their monthly payments will go down.

6. *The offer*. An offer is always a good idea and should represent a specific reason to call now, such as "Limited supply."

7. *Your company name and logo*. Although this needs to be on the mailer, it shouldn't overshadow the offer.

8. *Call to action*. Tell prospects exactly what you want them to do. Example: "Call today for more information" or "See us online."

9. *Contact information*. Provide your name, phone number, and web address directly following the call to action. Whatever you ask prospects to do, give them a way to do it easily.

Source: Joe Niewierski, vice president, marketing, PostcardMania (www.post cardmania.com), Clearwater, Fla.

5 Great Sources for Mailing Lists

The best-looking direct mail piece is useless if you have nowhere to send it. Here are sources for compiling your mailing list.

1. *Your children's sports organizations*. Let your fellow "soccer moms" and "softball dads" know you're in real estate.

2. *Local employer staff lists*. Employers, such as large hospitals, often publish employee magazines or newsletters. If you can purchase the roster, you'll get exposure to a large number of professionals in the area. In the case of a hospital, it's an essential step if you specialize in serving the real estate needs of medical professionals.

3. *Chambers of commerce.* Your local chamber may have lists of specialty groups that fit your niche, such as attorneys or minority business owners. Depending on the chamber's guidelines, you can purchase a list directly or consider advertising in the chamber's publication and get a list as part of the advertising fee.

4. *Universities and colleges.* Institutions of higher learning often have lists of entrepreneurs and alumni in certain geographical regions. Check with the public affairs department at your local institutions or your alma mater for the availability of this information.

5. *Your place of worship or other nonprofit organization to which you belong.* You probably have a membership roster. Let other members know that if they buy or sell a home through you, you'll donate a percentage of your commission back to the group.

Source: Greg Herder, Hobbs/Herder Advertising (www.hobbsherder.com), Newport Beach, Calif.

4 Audiences Your Web Site Should Reach

To guarantee an online marketing payoff, post content that consumers find critical—even when they're not actively in the market to sell or buy. Your site should target:

1. *Current home buyers.* Create and operate an IDX (Internet data exchange) site to post listings in your area included in the IDX data feed provided by your MLS, and also include on the site information such as a mortgage guide, school and neighborhood information (try eNeighborhoods,

www.eneighborhoods.com), a real estate glossary (available free at http://realestateglossary.internetcrusade.com), and frequently asked questions about the home buying and selling process.

2. *Past clients and others in your sphere of influence.* Include lists of service providers in the area (plumbers, landscapers, pool cleaners, maintenance people) and set up a place for members of the community to post news about local events.

3. *Potential clients.* Post your resume and qualifications—including testimonials—and your full contact information.

4. *Property owners.* Create a database of information on the latest rental property news and procedures.

Once you have great content, it's just as critical to get people to see it. Make your web site part of your comprehensive marketing strategy. Include your URL on your letterhead and business cards, in advertisements, and on all other marketing materials. And don't forget to talk it up to everyone you meet.

Source: Saul Klein, InternetCrusade (www.internetcrusade.com), San Diego.

🏠 *5 Steps to Building an Inner Circle*

Win referrals by cultivating an inner circle of allied resources.

1. *Prepare a list that includes loyal contacts,* including prospects, partners, vendors, local practitioners, and practitioners you know outside your area.

2. *Make systematic personal contact* through direct mail, newsletters, phone calls, drop-ins, lunches, or parties.

3. *Follow up with special communications*, such as handwritten notes, gifts, or endorsement letters from third parties.

4. *Develop customer loyalty* with great service, a caring attitude, and good communication.

5. *Implement a client-appreciation program* that demonstrates you go the extra mile every month.

Adapted from *The Millionaire Real Estate Agent* (McGraw-Hill, 2004) by Gary Keller with Dave Jenks and Jay Papasan. Copyright © 2004 by Rellek Publishing Partners.

Teach the Children Well

A great way to help students get off on a sound financial footing—and create name recognition among future homeowners—is to offer free seminars to high school and college students. Working with students can be personally rewarding, too. For more than 15 years, the Colorado Association of REALTORS® has offered a high school curriculum called "It's Your Move." Among the topics are:

Finding an Apartment

Furnished or unfurnished?

Inspecting the apartment.

Lease application.

Tenant and landlord rights and responsibilities.

Discrimination in housing.

Renter's insurance.

Role of the Real Estate Practitioner

What's a REALTOR®?

The real estate broker.

The real estate sales associate.

Duties and services of a real estate agent.

The broker's role in the community and the housing industry.

Buying a House

Exploring the market.

Checking the property.

The real estate sales contract.

Types of loans.

Closing the deal.

Keeping house records.

Selling a House

Changes in value.

Sell or remodel?

Adding space.

Modernizing.

Credit

The importance of good credit.

Credit scores.

What impacts credit?

Tips for maintaining good credit.

Source: Colorado Association of REALTORS®, Englewood, Colo.

Make the Tool Fit the Goal

Too many real estate pros confuse marketing with selling. Marketing represents a first step: establishing a personal connection. Selling is the follow-up. Effective marketing stimulates people's curiosity to call you. Here's how to use key marketing tools.

Personal Brochure

- Great for . . . Giving prospects a snapshot of your credentials and values. Your "story" should help to build relationships. It's best used in conjunction with other marketing tools.

- Watch out . . . Poor quality printing, photographs, or content will damage rather than enhance your reputation. Unrealistic promises will send readers running. Don't tell buyers you can get them the best value and then, in the next paragraph, tell sellers you'll get them the best price. Readers will catch the contradiction.

Billboard

- Great for . . . Reinforcing name identity if used over several months and with other tools.

- Watch out . . . Billboards can be expensive and tend to work best for big players.

Personalized Ad

- Great for . . . Making a call to action that helps build a relationship, if repeated over time, perhaps twice a month for at least six months.

- Watch out . . . It takes at least six months for an ad to work its magic, so it's relatively expensive. Once you commit to this strategy, you have to keep it going to produce results.

Web Site

- Great for . . . Giving you credibility, providing local information, and generating listings.

- Watch out . . . If your site tries to compete with national web sites and offer global information, it may fail to capitalize on what sets you apart—local expertise. Also, no matter how current your market knowledge, if your site isn't regularly updated, prospects won't believe you are, either.

Source: Greg Herder, Hobbs/Herder Advertising (www.hobbsherder.com), Newport Beach, Calif.

5 Ways to Make a Big Impact with Video

Video has gone from a nice-to-have to need-to-have for web sites, particularly in real estate.

1. *Welcome online visitors.* Create a video that automatically plays to greet new visitors to your web site and to tell them how to take advantage of all the tools and resources you provide. Work with your web designer to make sure the video plays only for those who have never visited your site before. Otherwise, you risk annoying repeat visitors.

2. *Provide interactive tutorials.* Some visitors won't be as savvy as others when it comes to using the home search tools and other resources you've made available online. Avoid time-consuming calls about how to use your site by offering a step-by-step video tutorial that can be accessed with the click of a mouse.

3. *Tour listings.* Video provides a more realistic perspective of a home than photos alone. With video, you can also add background music or a narrative to guide the viewer through each room and talk about special features.

4. *Tour the neighborhood*. Buyers often consider the community just as important as the home itself. Take viewers on a tour of local parks, schools, and museums.

5. *Show them how to stage*. Keep sellers coming back to your site by offering short videos that instruct them on the various aspects of preparing a home for sale. Include clips of a room before and after staging.

Compiled by REALTOR® Magazine's editorial staff.

Create a Successful Blog

Blogs—short for web logs—are online journals that give everyone the opportunity to be a writer and publisher. Real estate practitioners use the medium to interact with their community and reinforce their professional expertise. Here's how to get started:

■ *Understand what a blog can do for you*. Blogs are frequently updated and blend personal opinions and fact with links to other resources. If done right, your blog will showcase your real estate know-how and differentiate you from other practitioners in your market.

■ *Determine the purpose of your blog*. Before you leap into the world of blogging, find your focus. Your blog can be professional, fun, educational, or any combination of those. Define your blog's goal. Will it position you as the neighborhood real estate expert? Will it service your clients and prospects? Will it help you network with other real estate pros or with fellow hobbyists?

■ *Select blog software*. There's no shortage of programs that make it extraordinarily simple to create and update a blog.

With no more effort or time than it takes to compose an e-mail, you can have your latest blog entry on the web. Experiment with different software programs, such as Google's Blogger (www.blogger.com) or InternetCrusade's RealTown Blogs (www.realtownblogs.com), both of which are free.

■ *Address the needs of your target audience.* Think of yourself as an editor who must provide compelling and relevant news and filter information on your audience's behalf. For example, if your audience is primarily buyers, use your blog to deliver buying tips and information on properties just minutes after they hit the market.

■ *Update your blog regularly.* Create a schedule of when you'll add new postings, whether it's three times a day or once a week. Let readers know how often the site is updated, and stay true to your word. Fresh content will keep your audience interested and will help the blog rank higher on search engines.

■ *Encourage audience participation.* Ask for opinions and feedback on the issues you cover in your blog. For example, "Which architectural style do you like best?" or "What would you like to see developed at the corner of Main Street and Forest Drive?" Also include a "comments" section where readers can post other feedback any time.

■ *Jazz it up.* Add dimension to your blog with photos, videos, and links to news articles, relevant web sites, and your favorite blogs.

■ *Use RSS feeds.* A technology called RSS, short for "really simple syndication," allows you to proactively distribute your blog content. It works like this: People who visit your blog—and have already installed an RSS reader on their computer—can click on a link you provide to have the content delivered straight to their reader. A reader lets blog aficionados access all the blogs they subscribe to in one spot. Make sure your blog software has RSS feed capability.

■ *Arrange postings by categories.* Your blog software will automatically sort your postings on your blog site with the newest content on top. But that makes it difficult for visitors to your site to zero in on the topics they find most interesting. Use the "categories" feature of your blog software to organize your postings by topic.

■ *Promote your blog at every opportunity.* Create a prominent link to the blog on your web site, include the blog's web address in your e-mail signature, and reference your blog in all advertising and marketing materials. If you publish an article in your blog that you're particularly proud of, send a link to everyone in your sphere of influence. Be sure to have someone check your spelling and grammar before you publish. Errors will reflect badly on you.

Source: InternetCrusade (www.internetcrusade.com), San Diego.

8 Tips for Better Digital Photos

It's never been easier to impress clients with professional-quality photos. To take better shots:

1. *Know thy camera.* You don't want to be reading the manual and fiddling with settings when that once-in-a-lifetime moment appears.
2. *Overdo it.* With digital film, it costs you nothing to keep clicking. So try the same shot from different angles, distances, and heights.

3. *Increase memory.* Don't be forced to delete photos. Buy a bigger memory card. Cards offering less than 16 megabytes of memory are inadequate for many high-resolution cameras on the market today.

4. *Time it right.* Many digital cameras have a slight time lag between the click and when the picture is taken. Master the timing of your camera so that you don't miss the shot if it involves movement.

5. *Steady as she goes.* Even slight movement can blur your pictures. If you have a viewfinder, use that instead of the LCD screen to line up a shot. The farther you hold the camera from your face, the more likely you are to wobble it.

6. *Set it right.* If you intend to e-mail photos to clients or post them on your web site, set your camera to save images in the JPG format at the lowest available resolution (often 1 megapixel or one-quarter size). Higher quality settings will substantially increase the time it takes consumers to download the pictures. And because computer monitors can display images at only 72 dots per inch, a higher resolution won't give viewers a better picture.

7. *Reduce glare.* If one portion of the house you're shooting comes out looking too dark, your problem is probably underexposure, which often occurs when the background light is brighter than the details you're trying to capture. To reduce the impact of background light, take exterior pictures when the sun is in front of the house or wait for an overcast day.

8. *Find your focus.* If you take pictures through a window, the camera's auto-focus feature may zero in on a nearby object (the window screen or a tree branch) and not the intended subject matter, resulting in blurry photos. To avoid this, set

your camera's focus on infinity rather than on auto-focus or move the center of your photo slightly to shift the auto-focus away from the object that's confusing it.

Parting shots: Once you've mastered camera technique, take your camera to closings. Photograph the buyers in the waiting room, signing the documents, and holding the keys as they smile from ear to ear. E-mail them the pix along with your name and contact info so they can send the photos to friends and family—a handy way to build referrals. Always carry a spare battery. Without it, your camera will become an expensive paperweight.

Sources: Terry Watson, real estate speaker, Watson World Corporation (www .terrywatson.com), Chicago; and Stephen M. Canale (www.canale.com), real estate speaker and author, Ypsilanti, Mich.

8 Steps to Staging a Virtual Tour

1. *Understand the camera's perspective.* The camera's eye is very different from the human eye. It magnifies clutter and poor furniture arrangement. To make a home shine in a virtual tour or video presentation, cater to the lens.

2. *Make the home "Q-tip clean."* Because the camera magnifies grime, each room must be spotless. Don't forget floor coverings and walls; a discolored spot on the rug might be overlooked by prospects during a regular home showing, but that stain becomes a focal point for online viewers.

3. *Pack up the clutter.* But leave three items of varying heights on each surface. For example, on an end table you can place a lamp (high), a small plant (medium), and a book (low).

4. *Snap pictures.* This will give you an idea of what the home will look like on camera. Closely examine the photos and list changes that would improve each room's appearance: opening blinds to let in natural light, removing magnets from the refrigerator, or taking down distracting art.

5. *Pare down furniture.* Identify one or two pieces of furniture that can be removed from each room to make the space appear larger.

6. *Rearrange.* Spotlight the flow of a space by creating a focal point on the farthest wall from the doorway and arranging the other pieces of furniture to make a triangle shape. The focal point may be a bed in a bedroom or a china cabinet in a dining room.

7. *Reaccessorize.* Include a healthy plant in every room; the camera loves green. Energize bland decor by placing a bright vase on a mantle or draping an afghan over a couch.

8. *Keep the home in shape.* You want buyers who liked what they saw online to encounter the same home in person.

Source: Barb Schwarz, Staged Homes (www.stagedhomes.com), Concord, Calif.

6 Ways to Get Positive PR

Get reporters to tap your associates' expertise to explain the world of real estate. Positive PR lends your brokerage a lot of credibility. Here's how to encourage reporters to call:

1. *Know who's covering what.* Read the newspaper or magazine section you're targeting for coverage to learn who the editors and writers are and what they cover. Do the same thing for TV and radio programs.

2. *Keep your releases newsworthy.* Editors and reporters receive a lot of mail. Does what you're sending really warrant a news story?

3. *Offer ideas.* Whenever you're talking to a reporter, offer several additional story ideas.

4. *Provide useful referrals.* If you're not the best source on a topic, refer the reporter to someone who is. The reporter will come back to you for future pieces.

5. *Be a source, not the subject.* Single-source stories are rare. So when you're talking to a reporter, suggest broad stories with several sources. You'll have a better chance of getting a story placed.

6. *Don't double-place exclusives* (give the same story to competing publications).

Source: Emily Johnson, Taylor Johnson Associates (www.taylorjohnson.com), Chicago.

6 Weeks to the Perfect Buyer Seminar

Holding home buying seminars can be a great way to attract buyer prospects—but only if the seminars are well planned and executed. Here's what to do and when.

6 Weeks Out

■ Set the date and arrange for staffing at the event. You'll need people at the registration desk and perhaps others at the refreshment table or to help people find seats.

■ Create an agenda of topics to be discussed. Don't forget to allow time at the beginning for welcoming attendees and introducing speakers, as well as time at the end for questions. The seminar shouldn't be longer than 90 minutes.

■ Find a sponsor to help defray costs. Mortgage companies, inspectors, attorneys, and moving companies are all potential sponsors.

■ Line up speakers for agenda topics. Your sponsor probably will want to provide a speaker, but you're in control so choose people you feel confident will stay on topic and present useful information. In addition, find out what audiovisual equipment, if any, will be needed.

■ Reserve a meeting room and any AV equipment requested by the speakers. Don't hold the seminar in your office, because people might be reluctant to attend. Public libraries, community centers, and local banks often have meeting rooms available at little or no cost. Look for a central location with ample free parking.

■ Contact a caterer to arrange refreshments. For a Saturday morning seminar, have fresh fruit, light pastries, coffee, and juice. For an evening seminar, offer cookies, coffee, and soft drinks.

■ Send invitations and flyers to the printer. Include the seminar's time, date, and location; the name of the sponsor; the theme or topics; and RSVP information. Send the invitations to specific prospects and use the flyers for general marketing purposes.

4 Weeks Out

■ Develop an advertising and marketing plan. Tactics should include ads in local newspapers and free weeklies, a notice on your Web site, and flyers in public areas such as bulletin boards at grocery stores and laundromats.

- Obtain handouts from speakers and send the handouts to the printer with an estimated attendee count.

3 Weeks Out

- Start marketing the seminar. Invite people in your target market, as well as potential first-time buyers (or investors, if that's your focus) in your prospect database.

2 Weeks Out

- Set up a conference call with the speakers to review the agenda and make sure they're prepared. Use the call to get the speakers energized and to encourage them to promote the event.

- Send confirmations to attendees reminding them of the time and location.

- Prepare evaluation forms for attendees to complete after the event.

1 Week Out

- Remind the speakers of the date and location—and make sure they know how to get there. Ask them to arrive at least 30 minutes early.

- Confirm the meeting room, AV equipment, and caterer.

- Assemble handouts in folders.

Day Before the Seminar

- Call all "reserved attendees" and remind them about the seminar.

- Prepare thank-you letters to send to attendees the morning after.

- Prepare thank-you letters to send to speakers the morning after.

Day of the Seminar

- Everyone involved in hosting the seminar should be in business attire. Remember, this will be the first impression many of the attendees have of you and others from your office.

- Bring your "seminar box." Include these items: business cards, pens/pencils, two extension cords, outlet adaptors, duct tape, masking tape, Scotch tape, blank registration cards, name tags, scissors, magic markers (both broad and fine tipped), stapler/staples, paper clips.

- Prepare the room two hours before registration. Make sure the registration table is set up and chairs are arranged in a manner suitable to the number of attendees expected—U-shaped for small groups, rows for larger groups.

- Set up a wrap-up meeting with the speakers to gather feedback and exchange information and leads.

- After the seminar, ask participants to fill out an evaluation form.

Day After the Seminar

- Send thank-you letters to attendees and speakers.
- Send handout packages to those who didn't attend.
- Prepare an attendee list for speakers and send it out.

3 Days After the Seminar

- Hold a wrap-up meeting to review participant evaluations and talk about what went well and what didn't.

- Contact attendees and ask for an appointment to further discuss their property needs.

- Start setting up your next seminar.

Source: Peter R. West, Premier Realty Group, North Adams, Mass.

🏠 *Questionnaire: Qualifying Buyer Prospects*

Every salesperson has war stories about indecisive, demanding, disloyal, or financially irresponsible buyers. This questionnaire can help you determine buyers' motivation upfront. Buyers who can't answer the questions definitively may not be ready to move into your hot-prospects list.

1. How long have you been looking?

2. Are you working with another salesperson or broker? If yes, whom?

3. Do you rent or own your current home?

4. What is your monthly rent or mortgage payment?

5. Must you sell a home before buying? If yes, what is the status?

6. Must you complete a lease period before buying? If yes, how long is the lease?

7. Do you have a budget for monthly payments? If yes, how much?

8. What's your price range?

9. Has a lender prequalified you for a loan? If yes, for how much?

10. How much cash do you want to use for the purchase?

11. Do you have special requirements in a property? If yes, please list.

12. If you have school-age children, are you willing to move during the school year?

13. Who is your employer?

14. Will anyone else help you make the buying decision? If yes, who?

15. If we find the right property, are you prepared to make a decision now?

16. What times are best to contact you?

17. What times are best to view properties?

18. How do you like to communicate (phone, fax, mail, e-mail)?

Source: Walter Sanford, Sanford Systems and Strategies (www.waltersanford .com), Kankakee, Ill.

Chapter 2

SELLING

Gain Clients for Life

G et a listing and you might think you're home free. Hardly, though that represents an important step. Before you toast the closing, you have other hurdles to overcome.

You need to price the home realistically, maximize its condition, and help sellers understand comparables in light of current and past interest rates and the economy at the time, says Sarah Funt, a salesperson with the Bethesda, Maryland, office of Long & Foster Real Estate Inc.

You also need to develop an innovative marketing plan, and possibly revise it and the listing price if the economy dips and inventory rises. But you're also the one who gets to share good news when an offer is made.

Along the way, you're wise to keep delivering some old-fashioned TLC. "You can't just sell and tell; you need to ask and listen so that you really establish a dialogue and rapport," says Bill Barrett, head of Bill Barrett Seminars in Orlando, Florida, and author of *Recruiting New and Experienced Sales Associates*.

The reason you have so many job responsibilities is that you're not just in competition with other salespeople and brokers, but with the best, most innovative service providers at hotels, restaurants, high-tech companies, and other businesses, all of whom keep raising the bar on consumers' service expectations, Barrett says.

Consider just one way you can top sellers' expectations: Instead of helping clients debate whether to make repairs requested by buyers because of the inspection, jump-start the process early on. Have them hire an inspector *before* they list. "If some roof slates are missing, they can make repairs affordably rather than wait for a bad report to suggest the entire roof be replaced," Barrett says.

Throughout the selling process, communicate, provide feedback, and cooperate with the other side, since you share the same goal—to get the house sold, says Joe Meyer, founder of Joe Meyer Presentations Inc. in Lake Grove, New York.

Even after you close, you still have some work. Ask clients for a testimonial for future marketing and stay in touch. Sarah Funt hosts an annual July 4 party for past clients, family members, and anyone who provided a referral. "I never take anyone for granted," she says. Adds Bill Barrett, "Your goal is to establish clients for life." Here's how to do so.

8 Steps to a Killer Listing Presentation

You'll have that listing in the bag if you:

1. *Prequalify sellers* about their motivations, their selling experiences, and attitudes. Are they truly ready to sell?

2. *Confirm the presentation* date, time, and location.

3. *Find out if the sellers use the Internet and e-mail.* Tech-savvy sellers may appreciate a laptop presentation; others may just find it impersonal.

4. *Prepare presentation materials,* such as a personalized cover letter, a list of your experience and skills, a brochure that includes information about your services and your company, team member bios, testimonials from past clients and customers, and press clippings.

5. *Learn as much about the property as you can.* Visit the home during daylight hours to assess its physical condition. Look up its previous selling price. Take digital photos of the house and include them in your comparative market analysis (CMA). You'll impress on the seller that you do a thorough job.

6. *Have a price or range ready* to suggest, and have comparables that back up your thinking.

7. *Prepare objection counters.* (See "7 Nice Ways to Counter Sellers' Listing Objections," page 53.)

8. *Go the extra mile.* Create an introductory videotape about yourself and your services to send to sellers before the presentation. Include a package of microwave popcorn.

Sources: Terri Murphy, *E-Listing and E-Selling Secrets for the Technologically Clueless,* 2nd ed. (Kaplan Business, 2000); Ralph Roberts, Ralph R. Roberts Real Estate, Warren, Mich.; and REALTOR® Magazine Online's (REALTOR.org/realtormag) Listing section.

22 *Listing Presentation Slip-Ups*

Before the Presentation

1. *Showing up late.* To make the best impression, be about five minutes early. If you get there more than 15 minutes early, you'll be considered too eager or too rude. If you're late, you've already blown the presentation.

2. *Smelling like dogs, cats, or smoke.* No seller will love your pet, or your cigar, the way you do.

3. *Not doing your homework.* Talk to the sellers before the appointment. You should know before you get there about the general condition of the home, how much the sellers are willing to do to get it into "show shape," and their motivation for selling.

4. *Not knowing the sellers' financial situation.* Do your due diligence before the appointment and know if there are any liens on the property or, worse, if the property is about to go into foreclosure.

5. *Treating the listing appointment casually.* Every appointment is a job interview. Rehearse your presentation regularly and have ready answers to common questions.

6. *Not visiting the homes in your CMA.* If you've previewed each of the homes you're using as comps in your market analysis, you'll be able to speak intelligently about the differences.

7. *Displaying architectural ignorance.* An owner who's particularly proud of the Tudor influences on her home won't be impressed if you have no clue about Tudor style. For a style primer, visit REALTOR® Magazine Online's Architecture Guide (under Tools at REALTOR.org/realtormag).

During the Presentation

8. *Moving too quickly.* Many practitioners advocate a two-step listing presentation. Use the first appointment to build rapport and view the interior. Then do your research, find the best comps, and come back to cinch the listing.

9. *Not tailoring your presentation to the audience.* You'll lose some Generation X or Generation Y sellers if you talk

about advertising their home in the newspaper without also talking about having a video tour, personalized web site, and e-mail marketing.

10. *Talking more than listening.* Don't become caught up in selling yourself. How can you help the sellers if you don't know what they want or need?

11. *Ignoring someone.* If you're meeting with a couple, don't focus on only one party. You may end up alienating the true decision maker. If you're presenting to older sellers and their grown children, also avoid talking only to the sellers or only to their children.

12. *Ignoring pets.* In some households, the dog or cat is a part of the family. If you ignore or show disdain for pets, you may offend the sellers. If you have allergies to household pets, don't let it be known.

13. *Not knowing the neighborhood.* Research all the homes that have sold in the area over the last six months, regardless of whether they're comparable, and be ready to explain why a recent sale isn't a good comparable.

14. *Failing to explain your systems.* Have a system and be able to share details of it with the sellers. That means outlining all the steps you take to market and sell property and the measures you put in place to make sure nothing is overlooked.

15. *Using poor-quality materials.* Presenting black-and-white copies indicates you aren't serious about your work. Use color and nice paper stock for all your presentation materials. Also, make sure your materials have a consistent look and reinforce your brand.

16. *Not preparing the sellers for the process.* You'll do a disservice to the sellers if you don't prepare them mentally for some of the inconveniences they'll likely experience after they

list the house: the broker tours, showings, no shows, last-minute appointments, and strangers looking at their personal belongings.

17. *Appearing disorganized.* Don't tell anyone you misplaced your cell phone, notebook computer, or BlackBerry, and don't shuffle through your papers to find the one document that illustrates your point. If you come across as dizzy, disorganized, scattered, or harried, you'll eliminate yourself from contention.

18. *Failing to recommend improvements.* Sellers look to you to provide expert advice for preparing a home for market. Be ready to counsel them on everything from curb appeal to making the interior of the home clean and presentable.

19. *Letting your cell phone interrupt the presentation.* Under no circumstances should your cell phone ring during a listing presentation. Your work is all about relationships, and the moment your phone rings, you tell your sellers that they aren't as important as the person calling you on the phone.

20. *Not being upbeat.* Don't let your own troubles be known. Convey professionalism, a great attitude, and enthusiasm, and focus on the business at hand.

After the Presentation

21. *Not mirroring the sellers' behavior.* Are the sellers all business? If so, don't start hugging and talking about the wonderful things you're going to do together. The converse is true, too. If you've built such great rapport that the sellers seem ready to make you godparent to their child, take a deep breath and give a hug.

22. *Forgetting to thank the sellers.* No matter how you think the presentation went, thank the sellers sincerely for their time and for allowing you into their home. Say you'll get back to them, and follow up in a timely manner.

Sources: Thom Brockett, Long & Foster Real Estate Inc., Bethesda, Md.; Howard Chung, John L. Scott Real Estate, Bellevue, Wash.; Jon Hunter, John L. Scott Real Estate, Seattle; Linda O'Koniewski, RE/MAX Heritage, Melrose, Mass.; and Terry Watson, Watson World Corporation (www.terrywatson.com), Chicago.

🏠 *7 Nice Ways to Counter Sellers' Listing Objections*

An objection is nothing more than a question that should be answered, says Gail G. Lyons, editor of the *Real Estate Sales Handbook*, 10th ed. (Dearborn Real Estate Education, 1994, and the Residential Sales Council).

1. *Talk through objections.* Say, "Let's talk about why X concerns you."

2. *Divulge your weakness early.* Then build answers into your presentation to objections you know sellers will have. If you suspect your youth or inexperience may give an older seller pause, proactively address the issue by noting some specific example of your abilities. For instance, "I realize I'm young (or haven't been in the business very long), but my listings are selling X days faster than other salespeople's listings." You could also quantify and compare your sales volume with other practitioners' if it's strong, or emphasize that you're working closely with your broker on transactions.

3. *Appeal to fairness.* Calculate how many hours you spend marketing the average home, including the time to cultivate

and take the listing. Also include the amount you spend on marketing, desk costs, transportation, telephone, and other expenses. This figure will give you a dollar wage you've earned. If appropriate, compare this to the average salary of the sellers. "I make an average of X an hour for my time. Considering that I offer you 10 years of experience and success and a high level of integrity, I think that's a fair price."

4. *Don't get into a timing issue.* If the sellers say they don't want to list their house until they've bought another one, ask: "Will you be able to make a down payment on the new home without the money from this sale?" Also, remind sellers that they may not be able to negotiate as good a price on their new home if they must buy it on the contingency of selling their current house.

5. *Don't seem inflexible, but refuse to get into a bidding war.* If the sellers continue to question the value of your commission and state that another salesperson has agreed to a commission reduction, return to the sellers' stated needs and remind them how you'll deliver on each issue. "Everyone must decide what he or she is worth. Remember the list of services and marketing efforts I described to you during the listing presentation. I'm committed to follow through on those just as I described. Can another salesperson guarantee that?"

6. *Ask what more they need to know to decide.* If a seller says, "I'll think it over," says author and marketing expert Danielle Kennedy of Danielle Kennedy Productions in Pacific Palisades, California, ask, "Is there something I haven't covered? Is there a barrier between us that I can break through now?"

7. *Focus on objectivity.* If sellers say they're going to list with a friend, remind them that "it's hard for friends to be objec-

tive about each other. Your friend will want to take your side and not tell you things you may not want to hear. Sometimes that can be deadly to closing a deal."

Source: REALTOR Magazine Online's (REALTOR.org/realtormag) Listing section.

🏠 *More Surefire Objection Stoppers*

Don't let these common objections stand between you and a sale.

1. *The price is too high.*

   Stopper: If you think the price is too high, what would you consider a fair price?

2. *The offer is too low.*

   Stopper: I don't really decide what your home is worth; the market makes that decision. In my opinion this offer reflects the fair, current market price.

3. *Your commission is too high.*

   Stopper: I'm an experienced salesperson who averages more than $X million in sales a year. I'm an experienced negotiator, who usually sells homes at X percent of full list price. I'm an aggressive marketer, who averages a sale in X days. I think you're getting a bargain.

4. *Another company will list my home for less.*

   Stopper: Real estate companies offer a range of commissions. My company isn't a discount company. Instead we've chosen to provide a full-service plan that sells your house for the highest amount of money with the least inconvenience.

5. *I'll only sell for X amount.*

   Stopper: I'm certainly willing to do my best to sell your home at this price. But I want you to agree that you'll be willing to reconsider the price if the home doesn't sell in 30 days.

6. *I'm going to sell on my own.*

   Stopper: Would you try to set your own broken arm, or would you hire a professional? I have expertise that you don't. For example, I have access to the MLS to market your property effectively to other salespeople. I know what documents are required to close a sale, and I can help you secure them.

Sources: David Knox, David Knox Productions Inc. (www.davidknox.com), Minneapolis; William H. Pivar and Richard W. Post, *Power Real Estate Negotiation* (Real Estate Education Co., 1990); and REALTOR® Magazine Online (REALTOR .org/realtormag).

9 Convincing Arguments to Justify Your Commission

When sellers balk at the commission you're asking, how do you convince them you're worth the money? Try these persuasive pitches.

1. Without a professional, you may not sell as quickly. Your monthly carrying costs—mortgage, utilities, homeowner's insurance, gardener, trash removal, and routine maintenance—could end up costing you more than the commission.

2. You're gaining an objective negotiator who'll work to get you the best dollars and terms possible in your market and in a timely fashion.

3. You'll benefit from my knowledge of competent home inspectors, architects, contractors, designers, landscapers—all of whom you might want to hire to get your house ready to list.

4. Your home will be listed on the MLS and promoted through my advertising and marketing campaign, which includes newspaper and magazine ads, our company's real estate TV program, special newspaper inserts, brochures, my web site, and REALTOR.com. Such exposure would be costly to do on your own.

5. You're getting numerous open houses, possibly three over the course of a 60-day listing. Costs incurred might include two directional signs for each open house (roughly $50 per open house), newspaper ads (about $300 per open house, depending on newspaper, length of ad, and number of days published), photocopied materials on nice paper ($15 per open house), coffee and dessert or other nibbles ($20 per open house), and 300 postcards mailed to encourage attendance (about $350, depending on type of postcard and postage). Grand total: $2,355 for the three.

6. I'll run a direct-mail campaign with colored flyers mailed first class. Grand total: $500 for an upscale listing.

7. I'm part of a relocation network that refers potential buyers moving to the area, so I can help you reach qualified transferees, who are among the most motivated buyers.

8. You don't have to run home from work or stop other activities to show your house. I might even vacuum or tidy up for you. "If I have to, I will, and I have," says John Stewart with F.C. Tucker Co. Inc., Indianapolis.

9. You're getting my services and creativity without sharing in my overhead—office lease, employee payroll, technology support, file management, telephone expenses.

Sources: Wanda Grabner, Ludlow, REALTORS®, Indianapolis; David Knox, David Knox Productions Inc. (www.davidknox.com), Minneapolis; and John Stewart and Robbie Hunt, F.C. Tucker Co. Inc., Indianapolis.

🏠 *30 Steps to Making the Sale*

There's nothing more satisfying to you and your clients than a job well done. Use or adapt this checklist for all your listings.

1. Have your client sign an exclusive right of sale listing agreement that cites the address of the property and sets the price, commission, length of the listing, and your respective obligations to one another.

2. Lay the groundwork for a happy partnership. Walk through the house with the sellers. Discuss and give examples of recently sold comps. Decide what improvements are needed before you show the listing. Learn the sellers' timetable to move. Ask if there are days or times when the house can't be shown. Recommend that the sellers write down concerns and set a weekly time to talk by phone. Agree on a preferred method of regular contact—by phone or e-mail.

3. Develop a marketing plan that covers when ads will run in newspapers and on the Internet and the frequency of broker and public open houses and special promotions.

4. Send the sellers a package within a few hours of their signing the listing. It should cover your marketing plan and

specify important documents that they'll need to provide, including a prior title insurance policy, up-to-date survey, invoices of improvements made to the house, the deed to the house, and a recent termite inspection, if applicable.

5. Arrange for photographs of the exterior and interior for a brochure, ads, and virtual tour.

6. Enter the listing in the MLS.

7. Send notification of the listing to top performing salespeople in your market whom you know have buyers in the market.

8. Check with your sellers to ensure they've completed necessary improvements previously agreed upon.

9. Focus on the exterior. Place a sign in the yard if the community or condo association permits it. Hang a lockbox if the sellers agree.

10. Arrange the first broker open house. Mail postcards, make calls to other offices, and order the food and beverages. Be sure the house is clean and staged correctly.

11. Ask open house attendees for feedback, and relay their comments to your clients. Have sellers make necessary changes. For instance, if people complained the house was dark, suggest adding lights.

12. Arrange an open house for prospective buyers. Place ads, put a sign in the yard, and check with the owner that the house is clean and staged properly.

13. Get feedback from attendees. Relay it to clients. Make necessary changes.

14. If necessary, set a schedule for additional open houses.

15. Report new feedback weekly. If interest is minimal, discuss a new plan or price.

16. If offers materialize, present them and consult with your sellers about their viability and acceptability. Ask the buyers' reps whether their clients are qualified and working with a lender, and request documentation.

17. Negotiate the best offer with your clients and the other side.

18. Execute the contract. Make sure all parties receive copies.

19. Attend inspections and be aware of valid problems that were identified, such as termites, a leaky roof, or defective air-conditioning or heating. Set a date for work to be done.

20. Get copies of receipts showing the work that's been done.

21. Arrange the closing. Send a copy of the executed contract to your closing agent. Monitor the process, from the agent to the buyers' lender to the underwriter and the title company. Make sure everyone complies with the contract's time constraints.

22. Sit down with your sellers to review the completed contract.

23. Be sure your clients have thoroughly cleaned the house before the walk-through. Attend the walk-through in case buyers have concerns or complaints. Work with the sellers to resolve problems before the closing.

24. Attend the closing, since more questions may arise. You want to know that all goes smoothly.

25. Be sure your sellers have notified utilities and paid final bills.

26. Have the sellers turn over keys for the house and garage, instructions and warranties on equipment and appliances left behind, and names of competent workpeople they've used.

27. Deliver a thank-you note and gift to your clients.

28. Add your clients' new address to your database. They're a good source of referrals and future business.

29. Set a schedule to keep in touch with your clients, and stick to it so they know you care.

30. Congratulate yourself on another job well done!

Source: Michael A.J. Bindman, Bindman Bruzas Realty, St. Petersburg, Fla.

🏠 *8 Ways to Get the Phone to Ring*

Not all advertising is created equal. Follow these tips to create promotional copy that works.

1. Before you begin writing ad copy, *list the five best features of the property* and the emotional benefit of each. For example, a fenced yard has the benefits of safety and privacy.

2. Spiff up your *e-mail marketing* by creating an HTML template, which you can easily create using Microsoft Outlook. Using HTML lets you incorporate colors, graphics, and even flash movies in your correspondence with prospects. And because text and borders don't shift around with the HTML format, your promotions have a much more professional appearance.

3. *Close your ads and promotional letters* with a statement encouraging prospects to act—for instance, "Call today."

4. *List just one phone number in your ad.* Then set up your phones to forward calls to wherever you'll be. Listing more than one number will confuse buyers, according to research by the Newspaper Association of America.

5. *Promote online information* about your listings on your yard signs as 24-HOUR OPEN HOUSE.

6. *Use no more than five large words on a sign.* You have only four to seven seconds to get your message across as drivers pass by.

7. *Add a "unique features" section* to your property information sheet to highlight special or especially desirable features of a home.

8. *Consider running ads* in the Monday paper. It's usually thinner than the Sunday edition, so your ad won't be overlooked.

Sources: Valerie Hunter-Kelly, Keller Williams Realty, Clarksville, Tenn.; Sam Miller, Coldwell Banker Kasey & Associates, Hendersonville, N.C.; Mary Ellen Randall and Jamie Edwards, *Real Estate Advertising Made Easy* (Plan-It for Profit and Fun Inc., 1987); and Barb Schwarz, *How to List and Sell Residential Real Estate Successfully* (South-Western Educational Publishing, 1995).

Improve Your Ad Copy—Now!

Ads should make you want to see a listing rather than send you running in the opposite direction. Consider these two descriptions of the same house. Which one works better?

Cute, charming home   Red brick, 2-story, fresh with living space for all, 3 BRs, 2.5 baths. $425,000. Bring all offers. www.yourcompanyname.com, Realty Co.,123-REALTYCO.

Fabulous find!   Darling 2-story home in mint condition with 3 BRs, 2.5 baths, newish kitchen, family room with fireplace and access to patio, 2-car garage. Classic red brick. Great schools, great price. $424,500. See it now! www.yourcompanyname.com, Realty Co., 123-REALTYCO.

The second ad is far more compelling. Amenities are spelled out, and the ad highlights what many homeowners desire. It also urges them to visit sooner rather than later since the listing may sell quickly. The description is less vague and avoids euphemisms. "Cute" and "charming" often connote small and quaint. "Fabulous find!" says what's most important to many prospects today—a good value for their dollars.

Strong ads use active voice, create vivid images, aren't repetitive, avoid jargon, and are proofread carefully to catch grammatical and spelling errors. They also anticipate questions that prospects might ask.

Source: Elizabeth Danziger, Worktalk Communications Consulting (www.work talk.com), Los Angeles, and author of *Get to the Point!* (Three Rivers Press, 2001).

Add Buzz to Your Open Houses

Your listing is more likely to be remembered if you:

- Advertise a cookie or brownie contest and allow lookers to rate—and taste—three brands you've baked or bought.
- Host a raffle and give a gift card for a favorite restaurant.
- Have a listing sheet available of area houses for sale with addresses, special features, prices, and photos, so shoppers can comparison shop.
- Add nice smells but not too much. Lemongrass won't overpower.
- Display photographs of popular neighborhood amenities, such as local parks and a recreation center.

Most important: Urge sellers to price realistically and offer a competitive commission. These spur interest more than food, aggressive marketing, and clean closets.

Compiled by REALTOR® Magazine's editorial staff.

12 *Open House Blunders*

Open houses represent a large commitment of your time—usually over a weekend. Make sure there's a payoff by avoiding these gaffes.

1. *Poor visibility.* Have enough signs to help people find a tricky street and capture drive-by traffic from all major streets surrounding the home.

2. *Insufficient directions.* In your advertisements and flyers, give specific directions that take prospective buyers past the nearby golf course or other desirable neighborhood landmarks.

3. *Competing events.* Make sure the date and time of the open house don't conflict with a major holiday or sporting event.

4. *No giveaway.* Provide an item of value, such as an article about a new coffee shop opening in the area or a new park being built. Or offer a promotional item, such as a pen, CD-ROM of other listings, or water bottle with your contact information printed on it.

5. *House tours.* Most people don't need you to escort them around. Many practitioners advocate staying near the front door so that you can greet people when they arrive

and debrief them as they leave. If you prefer to walk buyers around the house, safety experts recommend keeping an exit behind you to ensure you can make a quick getaway if you sense an unsafe situation.

6. *No safety plan.* Call a friend, the office, or a loved one to let someone know you've arrived at the house, and check in with the person during and after the open house.

7. *An empty briefcase.* Make good use of downtime by bringing office work, cards, or letters to tackle when no one's viewing the home. Be sure to put the work down when any prospective buyers arrive.

8. *No early door knocking.* One of the best ways to ensure success at an open house is to show up an hour early and knock on a few neighbors' doors. Invite them to view the home; even if they don't know any interested buyers, you may get other listings by showing your diligence.

9. *An unready house.* Make sure the lights are on, classical music is playing quietly in the background, dishes are put away, the yard is mowed, drapes are open, and floors are swept.

10. *Lack of knowledge about the neighborhood.* You should know about the schools, stores in the area, and distance to major destinations. If you know that it takes 12 minutes to get to the heart of the city from the house, you establish credibility.

11. *A halfhearted approach.* Even if you have a contract, a deal can be killed by buyer's remorse, loan problems, timing, or a dozen other factors. Don't become so complacent that you lose the opportunity to line up other potential buyers.

12. *No follow-up*. If you don't collect the names and contact information of the people who attend the open house, you're losing out on a valuable opportunity to foster relationships and promote your services.

Sources: Thom Brockett, Long & Foster Real Estate Inc., Bethesda, Md.; Howard Chung, John L. Scott Real Estate, Bellevue, Wash.; Jon Hunter, John L. Scott Real Estate, Seattle; and Terry Watson, Watson World Corporation (www.terry watson.com), Chicago.

5 Negotiating Tactics That (Almost) Always Work

1. *The silent treatment*. Silence makes most people uncomfortable. After you've made an important point, look directly at the other party, smile, and wait. The longer you go without saying anything, the uneasier the other person will become. Eventually he or she will say something—anything—just to break the silence. The response will often be unguarded and give you valuable information.

2. *The flinch*. The flinch is a small sound or facial expression that communicates displeasure. Although a flinch is subtle, it can plant serious doubts in the other person's mind. Try flinching in reaction to a monetary offer or when the other party starts the negotiations too aggressively. Don't be surprised if even the most experienced negotiator becomes more flexible.

3. *The deadline*. Deadlines keep situations under control and get results. Begin a meeting by saying you must leave in an hour. Then, whenever the discussion starts to slow down or wander off track, move things along by reminding them that you must leave soon. Use longer-term deadlines, such as setting a date when an offer will expire, to motivate people to take decisive action.

4. *The competition*. Mentioning the competition is a good way to keep the other side from feeling too secure. If you represent the buyer, remind the listing agent and the seller that the buyer also liked several properties in addition to theirs. If you are the listing salesperson, hint that another offer may be on the way. Don't lie, but don't miss the opportunity to use the competition to your advantage.

5. *The departure*. Preparing to walk away from the negotiation can get dramatic results when the other party is being non-committal or refusing to make a counteroffer. If the negotiation has reached a stalemate, start gathering your papers and packing your briefcase in a matter-of-fact manner. If you have read the situation correctly, the other party should quickly offer a constructive response.

Sources: Adapted in part from "Strategy: The Negotiation Game Continues," *The Empire State REALTOR®*, March 1997; and "True Negotiation: An Exchange of Satisfaction," *The Real Estate Professional*, Sept./Oct. 1990.

Securing the Buyer's Offer

The right house at the right price should prompt an offer to purchase. Follow these tips to help ensure that your prospects become buyers:

- Educate buyers. Reduce the fear of the unknown by preparing a chronology of events that occur during a home purchase.

- Prequalify buyers to know for certain they can afford to purchase. Being unrealistic ensures that they can't make an offer.

- Create a strong sense of anticipation for the one or two homes you think best fit the buyers' needs.

- Don't let your personal preferences prejudice you against a home that might be just right for your prospects.

- Listen to their objections. Let buyers voice their concerns. Don't jump to respond.

- Remind buyers of imminent life changes—job transfer, change in family size (baby or parent coming to live)—that necessitate their move.

- Paint imaginary pictures that help prospects visualize themselves in the home.

- Reinforce the buyers' feelings. Get excited if they're excited.

- Be sure you have all the decision makers present. If a parent or spouse needs to approve the purchase, bring them along to the showing.

- Give buyers some quiet time during the drive between showings to assimilate what they've seen. Don't overwhelm them with information or idle chatter.

- Ask for the offer. Sometimes that little extra push is all prospects need.

From REALTOR® Magazine Online's (REALTOR.org/realtormag) Negotiating section.

6 Deadly Deal Busters—And How to Beat Them

You work hard to get the purchase contract signed, but you can't relax even then. Deal busters are lurking. Be ready.

1. *Property appraisal is too low.*

   Response: If buyers don't have enough cash to make up the difference between the loan amount and the purchase price, work with the sellers to see if they'll take back a seller-financed second mortgage. (Buyers may refuse to pay the price, but in a hot market that may not be the best response if the buyer wants the property.) Make sure the existence of seller financing is disclosed to the lender and won't affect the buyers' ability to qualify for the first mortgage.

2. *Repairs required in the contract haven't been completed.*

   Response: Head off the problem by including a clause in the purchase contract that the seller will deduct an agreed-upon estimate of repairs rather than getting the work done.

3. *Sellers say they can't make the move-out date.*

   Response: If the buyers have the flexibility to stay put, suggest that the sellers agree to pay rent for the period they'll remain in the house.

4. *Buyers can't qualify for a large enough mortgage to buy the home.*

   Response: Insist that all buyers be prequalified before showing them homes.

5. *The buyer purchases a new car two weeks before closing.*

   Response: Explain to your buyer clients that big-ticket purchases before the loan is finalized can jeopardize their credit score and endanger the mortgage approval. (It's best to make this point as soon as the buyer's purchase offer is accepted.)

6. *The inspector finds mold in the home's crawl space.*

   Response: Many buyers want to run at the first sign of mold, but most types of mold are benign for everyone except people with severe mold allergies, according to the U.S. Environmental Protection Agency. Urge the buyers to get a mold specialist to assess the type of mold, its extent, and the cost of any remediation before backing out of the deal.

Compiled by REALTOR® Magazine's editorial staff.

5 Things to Do When Your Listing's About to Expire

1. Check your MLS for the average number of days on the market for homes comparable to your listing, and use this figure to demonstrate to the owner that the listing should be extended.

2. Complete another CMA to determine whether the price on your listing still reflects market pricing.

3. Discuss with your clients what you've done to market the house. Develop a new marketing plan with a different approach, and present it to the sellers when you ask for a renewal. And don't wait until the last minute to discuss a listing extension with your client.

4. Offer cooperating salespeople a coupon for free ice cream or a free cup of gourmet coffee if they'll call you and tell you what buyers said about your listings.

5. If you don't think you'll be able to sell the listing, let a trusted colleague know it's about to expire and earn a referral fee.

Sources: Bill Barrett, Bill Barrett Seminars (www.billbarrett .com), Orlando, Fla.; and REALTOR® Magazine Online (REALTOR.org/realtormag).

6 Tips for Handling Multiple Offers

Multiple offers are a wonderful thing, provided you handle them fairly and with finesse.

1. *Present all offers promptly* and in the order they were submitted. Don't sit on an offer because a better one might come along.

2. *Ask sellers beforehand* to let you inform buyers if there are multiple offers as a way to increase the final sale price. Be sure sellers understand that buyers may withdraw an offer if they know there are competitors.

3. *Present all offers in understandable terms*. Price isn't the only consideration. Discount points, settlement dates, down payments, contingency clauses, financing provisions, and repair allowances can tip the scales.

4. *If buyers won't respond realistically* to a counteroffer, use a reverse strategy of telling them that they should forget about the house.

5. *Select one offer to counter* and hold the others as backups if negotiations fall through. Provide a deadline by which the buyers must make a counteroffer so that other bidders will know when to expect an answer.

6. *If you don't think any of the prices are high enough, stall*. Often buyers will get nervous and raise their price if they know there are several bids.

Sources: Danielle Kennedy, Danielle Kennedy Productions (www.daniellekennedy .com), Pacific Palisades, Calif.; and REALTOR® Magazine Online (REALTOR.org/ realtormag).

13 Ways to Add Flair to Showings

A house must be clean and clutter-free to generate interest. Even more may be necessary to set the listing apart, particularly in a softening market. Here are some decorating and updating tips you can share with sellers that'll bring "wows" from today's buyers.

- *Add touches of luxury.* Bring in real plants in beautiful pots; the best linens; and big, white, fluffy towels.

- *Paint walls, trim, and ceilings.* Keep adjoining rooms in the same color palette to make the home appear larger and flow better. Hire professionals to paint mullions on windows and staircase spindles.

- *Use slipcovers on mismatched furniture.* It's an inexpensive way to create visual unity.

- *Replace mismatched or poor-fitting door handles and cabinet pulls.* Buyers rarely get beyond a knob that comes off in their hand.

- *Install bamboo floors in contemporary settings.* Bamboo is outpacing maple as the new light-colored wood floor. Forget parquet and veneered wood flooring: Parquet is still out of favor, and buyers are aware that thin wood veneer can't handle many sandings.

- *Refresh closets with organizers and paint them a neutral color.* Make sure closets are lighted and buyers can see the back of all closets and cupboards. Closets will look bigger if they're organized and not stuffed to the gills.

- *Identify wall spaces for large and flat-screen televisions.* They're a must-have for most buyers today.

- *Clean, organize, and paint basements, attics, and garages.* Many buyers pass on a home because of a "creepy" attic or basement.

- *Edit furniture and accessories, including family photos.* Less is more.

- *Install new light switch covers.* Most buyers interact with these during showings. Worn covers show inattention to detail.

- *Purchase the best quality carpet pad.* It can make any new carpeting cushy, and buyers love cushy.

- *Place a vase of fresh flowers* in rooms in which you want buyers to linger longer.

- *Show off windows.* A good cleaning (don't forget the screens!) will help to highlight the style of the windows, bring in natural light, and draw attention to great views.

Source: Leslie Banker, decorator and co-author of *The Pocket Decorator* (Universe, 2004); and Mark Nash, Coldwell Banker Residential, Central Street Office, Evanston, Ill., author of *1001 Tips for Buying & Selling a Home* (South-Western Educational Publishing, 2004).

5 Things Feng Shui Followers Will Hate

Feng shui is an ancient Chinese design philosophy that tries to optimize the flow of energy through any space—a single room, a house, even an office building. Proponents say properties with good feng shui meet your physical, emotional, and spiritual needs and bring you good luck. Buyers who believe in the principles of feng shui will avoid homes with the following characteristics:

1. A bathroom located in the central chi area, the area of the home where all of the energies are in perfect balance. Water is a metaphor for abundance and wealth. A bathroom, with all its many drains, located in the center of the house offers the possibility that the house's positive energy will literally go down the drain.

2. A spiral staircase in the center. The staircase acts as a vortex, pulling down the chi.

3. A staircase directly in front of the front door. Energy doesn't have time to circulate throughout the house. Instead, good energy goes right out the front door.

4. A location at a T- or Y-junction road with heavy road traffic. Feng shui aficionados would perceive that the house is being bombarded by the negative energy of oncoming traffic.

5. An excessively odd shape. Aspects of a home layout that are important in feng shui, such as a relationship or wealth corner, could literally be cut out of an irregular-shaped home.

Source: Buy Your Home Smarter with Feng Shui by Holly Ziegler (www.holly ziegler.com) (Dragon Chi Publications, 2004).

5 Feng Shui Concepts Sellers Should Know

To put the best face on a listing and appeal to buyers who follow feng shui principles, keep these tips in mind:

1. Pay special attention to the front door, which is considered the "mouth of chi" (chi is the "life force" of all things) and one of the most powerful aspects of the entire property. Abundance, blessings, opportunities, and good fortune enter through the front door. It's also the first impression buyers have of how well the sellers have taken care of the rest of the property. Make sure the area around the front door is swept clean, free of cobwebs and clutter. Make sure all lighting is straight and properly hung. Better yet, light the path leading up to the front door to create an inviting atmosphere.

2. Chi energy can be flushed away wherever there are drains in the home. To keep the good forces of a home in, always keep the toilet seats down and close the doors to bathrooms.

3. The master bed should be in a place of honor, power, and protection, which is farthest from and facing toward the entryway of the room. It's even better if you can place the bed diagonally in the farthest corner. Paint the room in colors that promote serenity, relaxation, and romance, such as soft tones of green, blue, and lavender.

4. The dining room symbolizes the energy and power of family togetherness. Make sure the table is clear and uncluttered during showings. Use an attractive tablecloth to enhance the look of the table while also softening sharp corners.

5. The windows are considered to be the eyes of the home. Getting the windows professionally cleaned will make the home sparkle and ensure that the view will be optimally displayed.

Source: Sell Your Home Faster with Feng Shui by Holly Ziegler (www.hollyziegler .com) (Dragon Chi Publications, 2001).

7 Tips for Working with Foreign Real Estate Buyers

With immigrants and foreign business entities looking beyond the coasts, the opportunity to work with foreign buyers isn't limited to certain markets or to practitioners who travel overseas. Here's how to succeed.

1. *Remember that foreign clients may know real estate but not U.S. real estate.* You need to explain local market conditions and

U.S. legal issues. But be careful not to talk down to them, cautions Gustavo Lumer, with Lumer Real Estate in North Miami Beach, Florida.

2. *Focus on clients from one or two countries,* especially when you're just getting started, suggests Carmela Ma, president of CJM Associates Inc. in Beverly Hills, California. In that way, you can become more familiar with the culture and establish a wider network of contacts more rapidly.

3. *Recognize that factors such as currency fluctuations and a need for market stability may influence buying decisions,* says Pius Leung, president of Charter Equity in Houston. Leung recalls a client who bought a building, left it vacant for three years, then sold it for about what he paid originally. Yet, the client was happy because the currency in his home country had devalued by 50 percent over that period. So just by parking the money in the United States, the owner had made a profit, says Leung.

4. *Take it slowly.* Recognize that some cultures require more consultation and time to make a decision.

5. *Develop a group of tax, legal, and other experts in foreign ownership* of U.S. real estate you can offer foreign buyers as a resource, suggests Ma. Once you're seen as a trusted adviser, offshore clients will often look to you for assistance in other parts of the transaction, such as finding legal advice.

6. *Help bridge differences,* suggests Alan Berger of Breslin Realty in Garden City, New York. Simple things such as converting a price from dollars to euros or square feet to meters can make a foreign buyer more comfortable, says Berger.

7. *Get your Certified International Property Specialist designation* from the NATIONAL ASSOCIATION OF REALTORS®' International group. It's a great way to acquire skills needed to

work with foreign clients and to network. "The CIPS net-work represents the best-kept secret around for making contacts," says Lumer.

Compiled by REALTOR® Magazine's editorial staff.

🏠 *International: 4 Important Rules*

The Internal Revenue Service (IRS) has regulations that affect the sale of real estate by or to foreigners. Before you serve this niche:

- *Know what constitutes "foreign" for tax purposes.* Individuals are U.S. residents if they have either a "green card," which admits an individual into the United States as a perma-nent resident during the current calendar year, or a "sub-stantial presence" in the country. A substantial presence is established when an individual either physically re-sides in the United States for 183 days or more during the year or meets the formula for residency over a three-year period.

- *Know that 10 percent of the contract price of a sale made by a nonresident foreign owner must be withheld for tax purposes under the provisions of the Foreign Investment in Real Property Tax Act.* This amount must be paid to the IRS within 20 days of the sale. A seller may obtain a qualifying statement from the IRS that reduces or eliminates this withholding requirement. Properties that sell for under $300,000 that will be used by the purchaser as a residence for a specified time period are also exempt. Sellers who've furnished a "nonforeign affidavit" certifying that they will pay the tax are likewise exempt from withholding.

- *Ensure that foreign buyers and sellers have international tax identification numbers if they don't qualify for Social Security numbers.* These numbers, issued by the federal government, appear on all tax returns filed by nonresident aliens and on forms that show withholding from real estate proceeds.

- *Don't forget cash flow.* If you collect rents or other income for rental properties owned by foreigners who aren't engaged in U.S. business or trade, you must withhold 30 percent of the gross income (before expense deductions) for tax purposes before paying revenues out to the foreign owners. The withholding amount can be less if the country where the owner resides has an income tax treaty with the United States.

Compiled by REALTOR® Magazine's editorial staff.

Score Points with Multicultural Savvy

By the year 2010, an estimated 80 percent of all first-time homebuyers will be immigrants. To avoid being left out of this growing market, consider these tips:

- Know how important punctuality is to your customers. People from Germany, Austria, and Switzerland are sticklers for promptness. But being 15–30 minutes late is generally quite acceptable to those from the Middle East. The Japanese may be consistently 30 minutes late, yet they expect you to be on time. Waiting for them is how you show respect.

- Make known your smoking preferences. Smoking is more prevalent and accepted in other countries than it is in this country. If you prefer that customers not smoke in your car or in your sellers' house, say so.

- Find out their housing preferences. The Japanese prefer newer homes. The Chinese generally want natural-gas stoves. Some Hispanics like stucco exteriors, tile roofs, arched doorways, and tile in their kitchen, which may be reminiscent of homes in their native country. Filipinos like homes that look expensive and opulent, suggesting a palace. Many African Americans like formal dining rooms for Sunday family dinners.

- Carefully plan transportation logistics. Many multicultural customers bring extended family members with them to showings.

- Don't focus on one particular neighborhood. You can't legally or ethically assume that people of a particular culture want to live in an area occupied by others from their culture. Disclose as much information as you can about various neighborhoods so that they can decide.

Note: Any discussion of cultural preferences risks stereotyping. There are differences within a given culture, and preferences can change depending on the degree of assimilation. In your eagerness to be sensitive to someone's culture don't run afoul of fair housing laws. Never direct an individual to a neighborhood or property based on membership in a particular group. Let buyers set the parameters.

Source: Opening Doors: Selling to Multicultural Real Estate Clients, Michael D. Lee, (Oakhill Press, 1999).

🏠 *6 Gift-Giving Tips*

A closing gift is often a well-received gesture. When working with clients and customers from other cultures, take care with your gift choices and timing.

1. *Bring a small, thoughtful gift when you meet with new customers.* It's expected in certain countries such as India, Japan, and South Korea. Beware: Giving a gift before the end of a business transaction may be considered bribery in some cultures.

2. *Never outspend your clients or customers when exchanging gifts, so they don't lose face.* One strategy is to open your gift first, and then say you need to retrieve their gift from your car. You can have several wrapped and ready in different price ranges.

3. *Avoid giving gifts bearing the American eagle to customers from China and Saudi Arabia.* The eagle is a bad-luck symbol in those cultures.

4. *Never give anyone who's Islamic alcohol.* Most people who practice this faith don't drink. (Some practitioners advise against giving alcohol as a gift at all, to anyone, because many people don't drink.)

5. *Avoid giving Asian customers knives or scissors.* Anything that cuts symbolizes the severing of a relationship.

6. *Exercise caution when giving flowers.* In Mexico and Brazil, purple flowers are associated with death. White flowers have a similar connotation in Japan.

Note: Any discussion of cultural preferences risks stereotyping. There are differences within a given culture, and preferences can change depending on the degree of assimilation.

Source: Opening Doors: Selling to Multicultural Real Estate Clients, Michael D. Lee (Oakhill Press, 1999).

GIVE CUSTOMERS WHAT THEY WANT

Research from the NATIONAL ASSOCIATION OF REALTORS® sheds light on how buyers and sellers choose a real estate practitioner and what they expect from the relationship.

Most important factors in choosing a practitioner	FOR BUYERS	FOR SELLERS
Professional reputation	41%	57%
Knowledge of the neighborhood	24%	17%
Association with a particular company	7%	6%
Other	28%	20%

What they want most from their practitioner	SELLERS
Help finding a buyer for their home	28%
Help selling the home within a specific time frame	27%
Help pricing the home competitively	17%
Advice on how to fix up home to sell it for more	12%
Help with paperwork/inspections/preparing for settlement	7%
Other	9%

What they want most from their practitioner	BUYERS (repeat)
Help finding the right home to purchase	60%
Help with price negotiations	10%
Help with paperwork	10%
Help determining what comparable homes are selling for	10%
Other	10%

Source: 2005 NATIONAL ASSOCIATION OF REALTORS® Profile of Home Buyers and Sellers.

🏠 5 Credit Mistakes Buyers Can Avoid

Giving top-notch service to buyers starts with making sure they're on solid footing to obtain a home loan. Help them bypass these common credit mistakes.

1. *Not leaving enough time to fix errors.* Consumers should review their credit report at least once a year. Inaccuracies aren't uncommon, and it takes time to set the record straight. Each of the three major credit reporting agencies—Equifax, Experian, and TransUnion—provides one free credit report per year (www.annualcreditreport.com). There's a charge, typically about $15, to see the actual credit score, but the cost is worth it.

2. *Changing spending behavior.* A surprisingly good credit score can tempt prospective home buyers to open credit card accounts or take out a loan for a new car. Such actions can damage their credit score during a critical time, making it harder to obtain the loan they want.

3. *Seeking a subprime loan.* Even those with a marginal credit score can qualify for conventional loans. Tell customers to apply for the best mortgage loan they can find and to remember that other factors besides their credit score, such as the size of their down payment, come into play when applying for a loan.

4. *Confusing "prequalified" for "preapproved."* Prequalification doesn't require the lender to verify income and means very little in terms of a consumer's ability to obtain a mortgage. Encourage customers to get preapproved, a process in which the lender checks employment history, income, and bank funds, and reviews the credit report.

5. *Forgetting about credit after the purchase*. Your customers moved into their new home, happy they'll never have to worry about credit scores again. Not so fast. If they decide to refinance or move, their credit will once again take center stage. Remind customers to keep their credit score in mind as they deal with the expenses of being a homeowner.

Source: David Reed, CD Reed Mortgage Bankers, Austin, Texas, and author of *Mortgages 101: Quick Answers to Over 250 Critical Questions About Your Home Loan (AMACOM, 2004).*

7 Home Inspection Myths

An estimated 70 percent of all homes sold annually receive a home inspection. Still, confusion persists over what the process does, and doesn't, involve. Here are seven common misconceptions:

1. *Licensing ensures a professional home inspection.*

Wrong. More than 30 states have some form of inspector regulation—but state requirements vary widely. Verifying the inspector's credentials, experience, and adherence to professional standards is still important, even in a state with licensing.

2. *A home inspection is designed to identify problems that might be the basis for renegotiating the purchase offer.*

Wrong. The inspector's service is primarily one of education, providing buyers with a better understanding of the physical condition of the home and giving them the knowledge to make smart decisions. The inspector's observations or recommendations might help to dispel buyer anxieties and provide useful home repair and maintenance suggestions. When areas of concern or problems are identified, the inspector should play no role in fixing them or addressing them with the seller.

3. *Home inspections are needed for existing homes only.*

Wrong. New construction is often the most in need of a thorough inspection. Many professionals offer "phase inspections" in which the property can be checked at various stages of completion.

4. *Having an appraisal, code inspection, and termite or other hazard inspection eliminates the need for a separate home inspection.*

Wrong. Although each of these inspections is valuable, these should never be used in place of a complete home inspection. Similarly, a home inspection should never take the place of other prescribed inspections. To suggest otherwise is dangerous for your client and creates serious risk for you.

5. *Home inspections are for the buyer.*

It's true, most inspections are conducted on buyers' behalf during the purchase process, but prelisting inspections for sellers also can be beneficial. Prelisting inspections can identify areas of concern to be addressed before the sale and can assist in disclosure matters. The American Society of Home Inspectors recommends that a home be inspected every 10 years, regardless of whether a sale is taking place.

6. *Home inspectors are too nitpicky and will identify every little problem in the home.*

A professional home inspection is an objective examination of the condition of the visible and accessible components of a home on the day of the inspection. Professional home inspectors don't point out every small problem or defect in a home. Minor or cosmetic flaws, for example, should be apparent without the aid of a professional.

7. *All home inspector certification and credentialing programs are equal.*

Wrong. Some organizations for inspectors offer credentials in return for nothing more than an annual payment; other certifications are new or exist mainly online. When selecting a home inspector, look at the background, history, and reputation of the person's certifying organization.

Source: American Society of Home Inspectors (www.ashi.org), Des Plaines, Ill.

Top 10 Things Buyers Want to Know About a House

Don't waste your money putting unwanted info into your ads. Here's what will get buyers to call.

1. Location and neighborhood.
2. Price or price range.
3. Appearance (include a picture).
4. Layout or floor plan.
5. Total number of rooms.
6. Number of bedrooms and bathrooms.
7. Size of lot and square footage of house.
8. Details about the community.
9. Amenities and features.
10. Clear and simple contact information. Avoid a laundry list of phone numbers and e-mail addresses.

Source: Newspaper Association of America's 2006 *Newspaper Advertising Planbook.*

What Your Business Budget Should Include

It's easy to overlook the niggling details that make up a budget.
Use this list to ensure your budget is realistic.

1. *Taxes.* You need to know up front what kind of dent they'll
   put in your income, so that estimated payment deadlines
   don't catch you off guard.

2. *Marketing and advertising.* This is a broad, potentially expensive category, so put thought into every penny you plan to
   spend on items such as brochures, signs, street benches, television and radio ads, mailers, and postage.

3. *Donations, both planned and unplanned.* Planned donations
   are those you make every year. To come up with a bottom-
   line number on unplanned donations, decide how much
   you want to allot—say $10 each for food pantries, Scout
   fundraisers, car washes—and estimate how many of these
   causes you think you'll contribute to over the year.

4. *Online services.* Include domain names, hardware and software upgrades, hosting fees, tech support, and data entry.

5. *Education.* Plan for any continuing education courses, con-
   ferences, or coaching sessions you'll attend. And don't forget the cost of meals.

6. *Car expenses.* Don't be stingy here. Factor in routine maintenance (tires, windshield wipers, oil changes), insurance, licensing, road service coverage, unplanned repairs, and, of
   course, gas.

7. *Dues and fees.* Be sure to budget for all your indirect costs of
   doing business, such as association dues, MLS fees, and insurance premiums.

8. *Wiggle room.* What if you suddenly want to try a new marketing technique, go to a seminar, or buy a handheld computer? If possible, leave yourself a little extra for spur-of-the-moment expenses.

Sources: Faye Copley, Schuler Bauer Real Estate Services, New Albany, Ind.; Jack McSweeney, Century 21 Midlands, Kearney, Neb.; and Andy Reisinger, Coldwell Banker Preferred Properties Inc., Lehigh Acres, Fla.

🏠 *12 Documents Every Transaction File Should Have*

Keeping a complete transaction file is a good way to minimize your liability risk. For every listing, your file should include:

- Listing agreement, including comparative market analysis.
- Agency disclosure forms, including dual agency disclosures, signed or acknowledged, if applicable.
- Property condition disclosure form, if applicable.
- Marketing materials, including newspaper ads and print-outs of online listings.
- Relocation or referral information, if applicable.
- Correspondence and phone logs with buyers, sellers, attorneys, other practitioners, and other parties involved in the transaction.
- Inspection reports, if available and applicable.
- Lead paint or other hazardous materials disclosure, if applicable.
- Copy of purchase contract and addenda.
- Copies of invoices for completed repair work required for sale, if available.

- Settlement statement (HUD-1 form), if available.

- Escrow account records relating to the transaction.

Source: REALTOR® Magazine Online's (REALTOR.org/realtormag) Risk Management section.

🏠 *A Dozen Ways to Stay in Touch After Closing*

Completing these simple follow-up tasks soon after closing will demonstrate to clients that you welcome long-term relationships, not just closed transactions.

1. Call within 24 hours of the closing to congratulate the client on the sale or purchase.

2. Send a thank-you note one week after the closing emphasizing what a pleasure it was to work with the client.

3. Notify the corporate client when the employee's transaction has closed, and send a thank-you note to the corporation's relocation coordinator.

4. Create a binder for the client containing copies of the paperwork, such as appraisals, inspection reports, warranties, and settlement statements, generated during the transaction. They'll remember you when they have to check this information at tax time.

5. Offer to provide referrals for household services, such as plumbers, electricians, contractors, carpet installers, landscapers, or appliance dealers. Offer a free consultation on the value of a home improvement project using *Remodeling Magazine*'s "Cost vs. Value Report" (www.remodeling.hw.net).

6. Send a customer satisfaction survey form two to three weeks after the closing to get feedback on customer reactions.

7. Ask the client for an endorsement or testimonial letter you can use in your listing presentations and on your web site.

8. Find out if the client has any friends, family, or business associates who might be interested in receiving a free comparative market analysis of their homes. —*Walter Sanford, Sanford Systems and Strategies (www.waltersanford.com), Kankakee, Illinois.*

9. Remove SOLD signs, if you're the listing salesperson. Be sure that you repair any damage the signs may have caused to the fence or lawn.

10. Set up a client file that includes personal information such as names, birthdays, ages, pets, and hobbies for the client's family.

11. Add your client's name to your newsletter subscription list.

12. Enter the anniversary date of the closing into your tickler file so that you can follow up next year with a card commemorating their purchase. Later, you can use this date as a tickler to determine when the customer might be ready to sell. According to *The 2005 NATIONAL ASSOCIATION OF REALTORS® Profile of Home Buyers and Sellers*, the average home owner moves every six years.

Compiled by REALTOR® Magazine's editorial staff.

Chapter 3

KNOW YOUR MARKET

When You Keep a Pulse on What's Happening, You Spot Important Changes

Y ou think you know your market well—where to find the best ice cream, how late the post office stays open, which streets get backed up most at rush hour.

But do you know the most important real estate trends in your target area that will help you attract buyers and sellers and offer them critical information and service? And do you know that what you do know may soon become obsolete? It's critical that you do your research regularly, rather than once or twice a year.

Consider the quickly changing St. Petersburg, Florida, real estate market. Before Thanksgiving Day 2005, many houses attracted multiple bids within a few hours of being listed. By mid-2006 many sat on the market 90 and even 120 days, says Michael Bindman, broker-owner of Bindman Bruzas Realty in St. Petersburg. "It was as though someone switched off the tap," he says. "It's not a bad market, just more normal than what the area had experienced recently."

Other changes affect buyer and seller decisions. Many North Shore Chicago suburbs were a ripe target for teardowns until recently when local city governments passed new zoning law changes, says Honore Frumentino, with Koenig & Strey's Deerfield, Illinois, office. That means buyers who wanted to build a house might have to make do with remodeling one instead. Longer ago, the downfall of Enron in Houston wasn't expected to impact the Chicago real estate market. Yet, it did since the company used Chicago-based Arthur Andersen LLP as accountants. "A lot of Andersen execs sold their houses," Frumentino says.

Your job is to find out about such changes early on so that you can counsel clients wisely. How do you do so? Check MLS listings, read local and national newspapers, listen to the news, get active in your chamber of commerce and schools, and network with professionals in other fields, including human resources execs, who often are among the first to know when a company relocates, Bindman says.

In his own backyard, an important demographic shift has been occurring slowly over recent years. The population is growing younger, resulting in greater demand for houses with more bedrooms, bathrooms, and pools, he says. When he can't find a suitable house for a buyer, he searches through his city's public records to find houses owned for a decade or longer by the same person, which means someone soon may be ready to move. He tactfully approaches them to spur a possible sale.

Today, more than ever, you have to be proactive and a bit of a mind reader, Bindman says. The following lists can be your crystal ball.

A Word to the Ys

The members of the Echo Boomer cohort, also known as Generation Y and the Millennials, are beginning to enter their home buying years. Do you have a plan for reaching them? Marketers consider this group, whose members were born between 1978 and 1989, to be the first true digital generation, meaning you can expect tactics such as online video, podcasts, and cell phone text messages to play a much bigger role in marketing campaigns aimed at them. In the grand scheme demographers have created, here's how Echo Boomers compare to their elder home buying counterparts.

	MATURES (61+)	BOOMERS (42–60)	GEN XERS (29–41)	ECHOES (28 and Younger)
Defining idea	Duty	Individuality	Diversity	Authenticity
Navigating	Right and wrong	Good and evil	Paradox	Shades of gray
Style	Team player	Self-absorbed	Entrepreneur	Self-invented
Education	A dream	A birthright	A way to get there	An important first step
Work	Inevitable obligation	Exciting adventure	Difficult challenge	"You're fired"
Managing money	Save	Spend	Hedge	Diversify
Future	Rainy day to work for	"Now" is more important	Unpredictable but manageable	Working for my big break
What "new" needs to be	Revolutionary	Novel	Interesting	Authentic
Overriding conflict	WWII	Vietnam War	Gulf War	War on terror
Social norms	Conformity	Inclusiveness	Diversity	Multiculturalism
Calling it cool	Hep	Groovy	Fresh	The Bomb
Networking	The Club	Woodstock	The office	Friendster
Archetypal misunderstood youth	Andy Hardy	Holden Caulfield	Ferris Bueller	Harry Potter

Source: "2005 Yankelovich MONITOR," from Yankelovich Inc., Chapel Hill, N.C.

Influencing Echo Boomers (ages 17–28)

The following table identifies the amount of influence each of the following items has on getting members of the Echo Boomer cohort to try a new product, service, or brand. The percentages represent the combined number of people rating each item a 6 or 7 on a scale of 1 to 7, where 7 means "extremely influential" and 1 means "not at all influential."

| | **ECHO BOOMERS** | | |
	Total	**Male**	**Female**
Base	868	429	439
Advice from friend or relative	58%	54%	62%
Sample or free trial	52	47	56
Manufactured by trusted company	50	49	50
Refund/rebate offer	41	36	46
Money-back guarantee	41	38	43
Expert recommendation	41	39	42
Coupons	34	28	40
Contribution to charity or cause	33	28	37
Television commercials	27	26	29
Counter or shelf displays	22	20	23
Magazine ads	18	13	22
Radio ads	16	15	18
Newspaper ads	13	11	14

Source: "2005 Yankelovich MONITOR," from Yankelovich Inc., Chapel Hill, N.C.

Generational Word Association

Matures	Boomers	GEN Xers	Echo Boomers
Outer space	Inner space	Cyberspace	*Trading Spaces*
Walter Cronkite	*60 Minutes*	CNN	Fark.com
Hi-fi	Walkman	Discman	iPod
Blacklist	Black power	Black linguini	BlackBerrys
Radar	Radical	Radicchio	Radiohead
Engagement rings	Mood rings	Belly-button rings	*Lord of the Rings*
Dr. Spock	Dr. Strangelove	Dr. Kevorkian	Dr. Phil
Milk and cookies	Milk and Oreos	Milk and Snackwells	Soy milk and PowerBars

Source: "2005 Yankelovich MONITOR," from Yankelovich Inc., Chapel Hill, N.C.

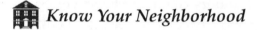 *Know Your Neighborhood*

You're new to an area, or you haven't kept up with neighborhood changes. How do you learn about the housing stock and what trends are occurring that may affect inventory and price? There's no single source but many.

- *Fire up your computer.* Start your day by checking the MLS for new listings and expireds. Begin tracking how long houses remained on the market and what they sold for.

- *Attend open houses.* Particularly if there's a lot of new inventory coming on the market, take time to see what's available and learn about restrictions. One building may not permit pets; another may have a history of special assessments.

■ *Learn the geography.* Buy good maps or use a global positioning system device to master getting around. Drive through new areas yourself before trying to navigate them with buyers.

■ *Sightsee.* Make notes of popular house styles and the proximity of stores, schools, and parks. Note FOR SALE signs, vacant land, and foreclosures.

■ *Talk to residents.* There's nothing as straightforward as information from those living in an area.

■ *Network.* Get to know area developers, architects, designers, contractors, zoning officials, and other real estate professionals. A developer may tell you, before word is out officially, that a 300-acre farm is slated to become a planned development. A lender may be able to explain an area's cycles.

■ *Be visible.* Join your chamber of commerce and National Association of Home Builders chapter. Attend your local REALTOR® association and city council meetings. Look into specialty organizations, such as the National Association of Women Business Owners. Go to planning and zoning board meetings to learn about building, tax, and assessment changes.

Sources: Stephen Beers, Keefe Real Estate, Lake Geneva, Wis.; Jeff Brooks, Real Estate Convergence, San Francisco; Marianne Curran, Realty World First, Raleigh, N.C.; Anthony Cutaia, Cutaia Realty Advisors, Boca Raton, Fla.; Gail Missner, Baird & Warner, Chicago; and Diane Saatchi, The Corcoran Group, East Hampton, N.Y.

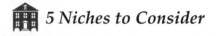 *5 Niches to Consider*

Focusing on a particular segment of the market lets you create targeted marketing materials and, in some cases, develop expertise in a particular property type—both excellent ways to differentiate yourself from your competitors. The niche you choose will depend on your interests and your market, but here are some ideas to get you started.

1. *Pet owners.* A survey by the American Pet Products Manufacturers Association in Greenwich, Connecticut, found that 63 percent of all U.S. households—69 million—own pets, up from 64 million in 2002. If you share a passion for pets, let prospects know you'll treat their furry friends right.

2. *Golfers.* There were 28 million adult golfers in the United States in 2006, up from 22.6 million 10 years earlier, according to the National Golf Foundation in Jupiter, Florida. Can you say golf course community?

3. *College students' parents.* The U.S. Department of Education estimates about 15 million undergraduates enrolled at a two- or four-year institution in the 2005–2006 academic year. The number of enrollees is expected to climb to more than 16.5 million by 2014. Help parents hedge high rental housing costs with a condo for Junior.

4. *Retirees.* The number of people age 65 or older will increase to 71.5 million by 2030 from 35.6 million in 2002, according to the U.S. Census Bureau. Cash in on the condo craze by selling empty nesters on the benefits of scaling back.

5. *Boaters.* About 71 million Americans, up from 69 million in 2004, participated in recreational boating in 2005, according to the National Marine Manufacturers Association in Chicago. Whether you're working the waterfront or targeting inland enthusiasts, you'll make a splash by understanding boaters' unique needs.

Compiled by REALTOR® Magazine's editorial staff.

15 Ways to Succeed in Different Types of Markets

Real estate trainer Mark Leader explains how to build business and impress customers no matter what "mood" your market is in.

When Your Market Is Slow

- *Work high-turnover areas.* Find niches in which there are more transactions than average for your market. For example, you may want to focus on a neighborhood of starter homes where there's a steady stream of first-time buyers moving in and growing families moving out.

- *Be realistic about pricing.* With a larger inventory of properties on the market, buyers can be choosier. Homes that are priced right will sell first. It's not easy telling sellers that their home is priced too high, but it's critical information.

- *Educate your customers.* Use market statistics and newspaper clippings to show clients that housing activity is slow. Tell them about ways to make their property stand out from the rest, such as by improving curb appeal.

- *Stay committed to customer service.* In a slow market, competition among real estate practitioners is fierce. Differentiate yourself from the crowd with top-notch customer service. Go the extra mile to make sure your customer is happy and to say thanks for the business.

In a Disaster-Prone Market

- *Know the risks.* Do your own research and talk with industry veterans in your area so that you fully understand the risks of working and living in a market that has a history of hurricanes, mudslides, floods, forest fires, or other natural disasters.

■ *Prepare a detailed disaster plan*. Be ready for the worst so that you can react logically, not emotionally, if a disaster strikes. Plan for your personal and business needs. Stock up on water and other essential supplies, and determine a standby office location in case yours isn't accessible. By being prepared, you can help customers stay calm.

■ *Turn your web site into a community information portal*. Tell customers that your web site will be updated with emergency information, important links, and community news if a disaster occurs. Make sure you account for this in your personal disaster plan so that the site will be ready for customers in need.

■ *Be honest about past situations*. Prospective buyers in your market undoubtedly will ask whether a disaster has ever occurred in the area or affected the home. The buyers are entitled to an honest answer so that they can make a sound decision. Explain what happened and how the community recovered.

In a Declining Market

■ *Be armed with market data*. Have up-to-the-minute information on market conditions so that you'll be knowledgeable at listing presentations and when talking to buyers. Give customers a clear view of what could happen if the market continues to decline. Don't paint a rosy picture; paint an honest one.

■ *Sell your company's services and success*. Wary customers need reassurance that they've chosen the best practitioner and brokerage to navigate them through uncertain waters.

Highlight your experience in similar situations and explain all of the resources your brokerage provides.

- *Price ahead of the curve.* If you've accepted a new listing, your sellers would be smart to price the home a hair less than what comparable homes on the block recently have sold for. By the time showings begin, it'll be priced competitively and have wider buyer appeal.

- *Become an agent of change.* Work with local government leaders and nonprofit development organizations to help jump-start a lagging market. Involvement in revitalization programs can drive investment and spur property appreciation in down-trodden areas. Positive media coverage is a side benefit.

When Your Market Is Crazed

- *Pay attention to details.* In a frenzied market, deals happen quickly and details can be overlooked. Deliver on your promises if you want to win repeat business.

- *Help buyers make their best offer first.* When multiple bids are the norm, it's important that buyers are ready to make a competitive offer quickly. Ensure they're ready with an earnest money deposit and that their financing is lined up. A down payment of 20 percent or more also can improve the odds that an offer is accepted.

- *Save 10 percent of your gross revenue for a rainy day.* If the market slows down, you'll have enough money saved to continue full force with your personal marketing, prospecting, and other business needs.

Sources: Mark Leader, Mark Leader Courses and Leaders Choice sales training program (www.leaderschoice.com), and "Agents of Change," REALTOR® Magazine, June 2005.

21 Hot Building and Design Trends

Housing styles remain fairly consistent, with certain styles more popular in certain regions. What changes are proportions of houses and their components—the materials used, the layout of rooms, and the rooms themselves. Many condo owners, for example, now seek amenities like well-equipped gyms and green space for people and pets. Other favorites are:

1. *Copycat materials*. New materials mimic old-time favorites but in lighter-weight, more energy-efficient versions. Dryvit Systems Inc. manufactures materials that replicate brick, granite, and limestone for outdoors and indoors.

2. *U-shaped designs*. When land is at a premium, a U-shaped house allows for a private outdoor space at the center.

3. *Hidden garages*. Fewer homeowners want to see a garage out front, even if they own a fleet.

4. *More color*. Splashes of bolder, deeper colors are in for shutters, doors, window frames, and even roof tiles. Historic colors are also popular. Color gives a more lived-in look, says Peggy Van Allen, color marketing manager for Dutch Boy Paints.

5. *Third-floor living space*. Since building up is less costly than adding on, houses are being designed to expand into attic space if zoning permits.

6. *Porches*. Back in vogue and deeper, porches function more as a living space than a passageway. Some homeowners want a private "sunset" screened porch off a master bedroom.

7. *Windowless media rooms*. In condo buildings where space is at a premium and windows are expensive, builders put media rooms, used mostly at night, in wide corridors.

8. *Green materials.* Interest in energy-efficient, sustainable materials is on the rise. Backup generators are popular for those in hurricane zones.

9. *Snoring rooms.* A bedroom that can double as a sleeping space for a family member who snores keeps that person from being banished to a sofa and a spouse from having a sleepless night, says Chicago designer Susan Fredman.

10. *Professional-style workout spaces.* No longer will a single piece of equipment do. Homeowners want larger rooms with all the bells and whistles for working out alone or with a trainer.

11. *Dual master suites.* Two master bedrooms with bathrooms allow families to accommodate older relatives or returning college graduates.

12. *Dual libraries.* With fewer living rooms built, more couples seek his and her libraries, or one for adults and one for kids.

13. *Cheese cellars.* Have a wine cellar? Time to add a cellar to age that bleu.

14. *Elevators.* For homeowners who don't want to move to a one-level house or can't add a first-floor bedroom, an elevator allows for aging in place.

15. *Multiples, multiples.* Two refrigerators have long been common; many are now opting for two dishwashers and even two laundry rooms, or two sets of washers and dryers.

16. *Media rooms.* Even in the mid-price range, some new homes feature an entertainment center outfitted with a projection screen, leather stadium-style seating, a surround-sound

system, recessed dimmable lighting, and a black ceiling, says builder Dennis Stilley of DGR Construction Inc. in Atlanta.

17. *Prewired whole-home systems.* A centralized panel that controls a home's systems, including the TV sound, security, thermostat, and lighting is becoming more mainstream as prices come down. Best of all: When you're away, you can carry a wireless tablet to check on systems or control them from your cell phone or e-mail, says Mike Whaling, business development manager for InfiniSys Inc. in Daytona Beach, Florida.

18. *Textures.* Whether in materials or paints, smooth is out and texture's in. Dryvit Systems produces a paint that comes in 80 colors, can duplicate textured surfaces, and is easy to clean. New York designer Liora Manné uses different yarns in rugs and blends colors. Rebecca Cole, another New York designer, recommends mixing textures such as slate, wood, and stone in the same room for a layered look, akin to layering apparel.

19. *Pet showers.* No longer located outdoors or in a laundry room, a shower for Rover may occupy a separate niche in an owner's shower.

20. *All fixed up.* More homeowners want to nix remodeling and buy a "finished" house, whether old and remodeled or spanking new.

21. *Ay car-amba!* Three-car garages have become common, and one company, GarageTek in Syosset, New York, says its average makeover is about $6,500. Makeovers often include paneled walls, tiled floors (sometimes with radiant heat), cabinets, shelves, lighting, a potting or hobby station, and

sometimes a place for a TV. "A three-car garage measuring 600 square feet is bigger than most rooms," says Barbara Butensky, director of marketing.

Sources: Peggy Van Allen, Dutch Boy Paints, Cleveland; Jeff Brooks, Real Estate Convergence, San Francisco; Barbara Butensky, GarageTek, Syosset, N.Y.; Erik Carlson, Dubin Residential Communities Inc., Chicago; Barbara Catlow, Dryvit Systems Inc., West Warwick, R.I.; Rebecca Cole, Cole Creates, New York City; Marianne Curran, Realty World First, Raleigh, N.C.; Anna Marie Fanelli, Floor & Décor, Tenafly, N.J.; Susan Fredman, Susan Fredman & Associates, Chicago; Lily Kanter, Serena and Lily, Sausalito, Calif.; Liora Manné, New York City; James Martin, The Color People, Denver; Ed Mattingly, Mattingly Custom Finishes, Chicago; Gail Missner, Baird & Warner, Chicago; David Robbins, Architecture Collaborative Inc., Ellicott City, Md.; Ron Smith, Orren Pickell Designers & Builders, Lincolnshire, Ill.; Emily Stevenson, New York City; Dennis Stilley, DGR Construction Inc., Atlanta; Sarah Susanka, author, *Inside the Not So Big House* (The Taunton Press, 2005), Raleigh, N.C.; Sam Switzenbaum, Switzenbaum & Associates, Philadelphia; and Mike Whaling, InfiniSys Inc., Daytona Beach, Fla.

Hot Foreign Markets

You run across a client or prospect looking to retire or buy a second home outside the United States. How can you help? To make a referral or to seek expert guidance on the tax, title, and foreign ownership issues in a market, search for a Certified International Property Specialist (CIPS) by country or specialization at REALTOR .org/international. You also can search by country for a Transnational Referral Certified (TRC) broker at www.WorldProperties .com, the official web site of the International Consortium of Real Estate Associations, which facilitates and sets standards for international real estate practice.

Here are the markets buyers will be flocking to if they aren't already.

Pacific Coast of Nicaragua

Pacific Coast property in Nicaragua remains one of the world's best bargains. This is dramatic coastline, with rugged shores, cliffs and rocks, crashing surf, hidden coves, and pinkish white sand. Residents enjoy the same beaches as in Costa Rica or southern California, but at one-quarter or one-tenth the cost, respectively.

Buenos Aires, Argentina

The Argentine peso, after nearly a decade pegged to the U.S. dollar, has leaped from a low of 19 cents to around 30 cents. But bargains still abound. For investors willing to move quickly, the opportunities in this cosmopolitan city are promising.

Dubrovnik, Croatia

A former city-state that once rivaled Venice, Dubrovnik dates back more than 1,300 years and is considered by many to be the Pearl of the Adriatic. With Croatia seeking membership in the European Union, prices are likely to climb in the next couple of years.

Montenegro

This small country in southeastern Europe borders the Adriatic Sea between Albania and Bosnia and Herzegovina. Prices are less than $75 a square foot, although Russian buyers have pushed up prices for oceanfront lots. In a good location near the shore, houses typically sell for $150 to $200 per square foot.

Panama City, Panama

Panama is typically categorized as a developing country, but the infrastructure, diversity, and sophistication of the country, especially in Panama City—with a metropolitan population of more than one million—tell a different story. The turnover of the Panama Canal in 1999 brought a glut of first-class properties to the market. Although the best opportunities are gone, prices are expected to increase for years to come.

Volcán, Panama

Located in the Chiriquí province in the west, Volcán boasts a springlike climate year-round, fresh mountain air, and beautiful scenery. Buyers will spend half as much to own here but will miss some of the amenities and infrastructure of nearby Boquete.

Chiang Mai, Thailand

Chiang Mai, Thailand's arts and crafts center, was founded in 1296. The land is a patchwork of misty hills, rice fields, and jungle, and the city's surrounding province is home to numerous hill tribes. It's possible to buy attractive two-bedroom homes for less than $50,000.

La Ceiba, Honduras

La Ceiba, the third-largest city in Honduras, has grown along with its ecological tourism and agricultural industries. La Ceiba residents enjoy Caribbean beaches, mountains, and rivers. Construction prices start at just $35 per square foot for a simple, wooden house.

Costa Maya, Mexico

The Mexican government is committed to transforming Costa Maya into its next great tourist destination by installing millions of dollars worth of infrastructure, including new roads, telephone and electricity networks, houses for employees, marina and beach installations, and docks for cruise ships. Property prices are on the rise and may one day rival the prices in Acapulco and Cancún.

Laguna Bacalar, Mexico

The Mayans believed this Lake of Seven Colors was a magical place. Today, Laguna Bacalar is an undiscovered gem. But, as development continues in the Riviera Maya region, this lake will begin to receive attention.

Source: International Living (www.internationalliving.com), a magazine devoted to finding the best bargains in international living.

Chapter 4

STAY OUT OF TROUBLE

No Joy in Getting Sued

Most women say having a baby is incredibly painful, but you forget the pain when it's over because of the joy the new baby brings.

Don't ever confuse getting sued with childbirth. Being sued is also extremely painful, but there's no happy feeling at the end. It's best to avoid litigation altogether. Unfortunately, "real estate practitioners continue to take legal risks until they or their colleagues experience the trauma of litigation," says Gary Nagle, a Juno Beach, Florida, attorney who concentrates on real estate transactions and litigation.

"And since there's no way to prevent people from suing you—it only costs about $250 to file a lawsuit—the only thing you can do is practice your profession so that you prevent people from suing you successfully," Nagle says.

The most important rule for practicing real estate that way, says Larry Chandler, CEO of REO Advisors Inc., which sells real estate errors and omissions (E&O) insurance in Coral Springs, Florida, is to make sure you put everything in writing. "If buyers or sellers have a concern about anything in a transaction, tell them,

'I'll be happy to write that in the contract for you,' " Chandler advises. But make the terms specific. "Have a specific time frame for the issue to be resolved," he says, "and agree on the remedy if it's not resolved in that time frame." Most important, if you add anything more than a simple provision, such as, "Sellers to leave dining room chandelier," make sure an attorney drafts or reviews the language. And don't change the preprinted portions of a contract form unless permitted to do so by your state's law.

To protect yourself if you do get sued, consider E&O insurance, which Chandler says is becoming more important because consumers and institutions are demanding it. "We've seen much greater knowledge by the public that real estate practitioners need E&O insurance," he says. "Many web sites recommend buyers and sellers check that salespeople are properly insured before they enter into a contract with them. And more and more institutions, such as mortgage brokerages, banks, and government agencies, are demanding the same coverage before they'll work with them," he says.

For more on avoiding legal trouble, read on.

Real Estate Law in a Nutshell

With so many federal laws and regulations governing real estate activities, it's all too easy to forget one or two in the heat of a sale. Here's an easy-to-use cheat sheet for some major laws affecting real estate. Be sure to check with your counsel about the specific application of these or other laws to your particular fact situation.

Do Not Call/E-Mail

Laws   The Telephone Consumer Protection Act of 1991, Telemarketing Consumer Fraud and Abuse Prevention Act, The CAN-SPAM

Act, and related Federal Trade Commission/Federal Communications Commission regulations.

Major Provisions Prohibits businesses—other than charities, pollsters, and political organizations—from calling individuals whose names appear on the National Do Not Call Registry (https://telemarketing.donotcall.gov).

- Allows calls to existing customers (those with whom you've done business in the last 18 months). Lists used for calling must be updated monthly.

- Allows you to call FSBOs only if you have a buyer for their homes but doesn't allow you to solicit FSBOs for a listing.

- Provides a safe harbor from prosecution for inadvertently calling someone on the do-not-call list if your company has written procedures on calling, provides training on do-not-call regulations, has accessed the national registry within the last three months, and maintains a company-specific list of numbers not to call.

- Allows real estate practitioners to send out commercial e-mail soliciting business if the e-mail is clearly labeled as a solicitation for business, includes the physical address of the sender, and allows recipients to opt out of future mailings.

Federal Fax Laws

Laws The Telephone Consumer Protection Act of 1991, The Junk Fax Prevention Act of 2005, and related regulations from the Federal Communications Commission.

Major Provisions Prohibits the sending of "unsolicited advertising faxes" unless the sender has an "established business relationship"

(EBR) with the recipient or written consent from the recipient before sending unsolicited advertising faxes. An EBR can be created either through an inquiry or transaction and doesn't expire.

- The sender must have voluntarily received the recipient's fax number. "Voluntary" receipt would include obtaining the recipient's fax number from the recipient's business card or letterhead, or obtaining the fax number from the recipient's public web site.

- The sender must provide the recipient the right to opt out of receiving future unsolicited advertising faxes, and the sender must honor opt-outs received from recipients within 30 days of receipt.

Lead-Based Paint

Law   The Residential Lead-Based Paint Hazard Reduction Act of 1992.

Major Provisions   (Applies to houses and apartments built before 1978.)

- Requires owners and their agents to disclose the known presence of lead-based paint in residential properties being sold or leased and to provide any available reports pertaining to lead-based paint hazards.

- Requires owners' agents to give all prospective buyers or renters a copy of the federal pamphlet, *Protect Your Family from Lead in Your Home*. It's available in several languages at the EPA web site (www.epa.gov).

- Makes salespeople responsible for obtaining a signed acknowledgment that the pamphlet was received and the buyer was provided with any available information about lead-based paint hazards or testing, and for keeping that acknowledgment for three years as proof of compliance.

- Gives buyers 10 days to have an inspection of the property for lead paint.
- Does not require that owners test for the presence of lead paint.

RESPA

Law   Real Estate Settlement Procedures Act of 1974 and U.S. Department of Housing and Urban Development (HUD) regulations.

Major Provisions   Prohibits real estate practitioners from receiving referral fees or anything else of value from service providers unless the salespeople actually perform a service that justifies the fee. Fees just for referring business are illegal.

- Prohibits practitioners or homebuilders from requiring buyers to purchase title insurance from a particular provider.
- Requires lenders to provide good faith estimates of closing costs and use the HUD-1 closing document.

Fair Housing

Law   The Federal Fair Housing Act of 1968 and its amendments.

Major Provisions   Makes it unlawful to discriminate in the sale or leasing of housing based on race, color, religion, national origin, sex, familial status, or handicap. Note that handicaps include physical and mental impairments, AIDS or HIV, alcoholism, or prior drug addiction. Some state laws also protect other classes, such as sexual orientation and marital status, from discrimination.

- Exempts "Qualified Housing for Older Persons," dwellings operated by religious organizations, and rentals in owner-occupied properties of four or fewer units (with the exception of racial discrimination).

- Prohibits salespeople from offering buyers and renters housing choices based on their membership in a protected class and/or a prospective area's racial, religious, or ethnic composition.

- Makes it unlawful to refuse information on available financing to persons on the basis of their membership in a protected class.

- Prohibits advertising that indicates a preference for or against any protected group. Note that this advertising prohibition applies even to owner-occupied properties with four or fewer units.

Compiled by REALTOR® Magazine's editorial staff with the NATIONAL ASSOCIATION OF REALTORS® Legal Affairs department.

5 Statements That Can Get You Into Trouble

1. "I've looked over the house, and I don't see any problems with water damage." Unless you're a structural engineer, never give a definite opinion on property condition. Encourage the buyer to seek the opinion of a qualified home inspector or other professional.

2. "I've seen this neighborhood improve since the city tore down the black housing project." Never, ever characterize a

neighborhood or home by one of the classes protected by the federal Fair Housing Act.

3. "You know, when I listed this house, the sellers told me they had to sell in a hurry, so you could probably get them to lower the price." If you're the listing agent, you owe a fiduciary responsibility to the sellers that prohibits your sharing confidential information with the buyers.

4. "I think you'll like this area. There are a lot of nice, middle-class Hispanic families just like yours." Attempting to influence a buyer's housing choice based on race, religion, sex, color, national origin, handicap, or familial status is called steering and is a violation of the Fair Housing Act.

5. "Since you haven't had any problems with water since you made the repairs, there's really no need to mention anything about the past problems to the buyers." Failing to disclose a material fact, such as water damage, that could affect a buyer's decision to purchase is ill-advised, even if the seller genuinely believes the problem's been remedied. The seller may, however, want to indicate on the property condition disclosure form that repairs were made on X date by X and that no further problems have occurred.

Compiled by REALTOR® Magazine's editorial staff.

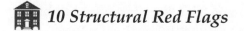 *10 Structural Red Flags*

No home is perfect. "Owners have reported to us that two-thirds of home inspections uncovered problems," says Dan Steward, president of home inspection company Pillar to Post in Tampa, Florida.

That's why many sellers decide to have a presale inspection. "For any homeowner, repairing problem areas before putting the house on the market can maintain or increase the home's value and avoid unpleasant surprises during the sales negotiation or at time of closing."

At the same time home buyers need to understand what's normal and what's not, says H. Alan Mooney, president of Criterium Engineers, a Portland, Maine–based consulting engineering firm that specializes in building inspections. "Most foundations have cracks, and 90 percent are normal," he says.

Help your buyer clients understand the biggest problems:

1. *Foundation cracks.* Ridges or lateral movement indicate a change in a surface that could be cause for concern. Remember, for the most part it isn't the width of the crack that's important, but the displacement of the surfaces on either side of it. Find out why the change occurred to get the problem solved properly. A foundation wall could be inadequate, or too much water may have accumulated outside.

2. *Load-bearing walls removed.* This problem may be tough for salespeople to spot unless the change caused ceilings to sag, ceilings or walls to crack, and floors to become springy. Pay particular attention to openings in basement and lower floor areas by looking for excess deflection in the middle of the span and cracks in the corners of the openings. A history of a home's renovation work may indicate that walls or columns were removed that should have been left.

3. *Faulty or insufficient wiring.* Again, this won't be easy to spot, unless wiring was done poorly or wires remain exposed. Have buyer clients ask whether wiring in older homes was updated and whether wiring can handle all their tech needs. A telecommuter might need extra capacity. A family with

teenage children might overtax a system that was fine for an older couple.

4. *Water, water everywhere.* Stains may indicate prior water problems, but so can surfaces recently painted to camouflage past problems. When you smell fresh paint, use your judgment to determine whether the house has been redecorated for sale or painted only in certain areas to mask a problem. When in doubt, ask the sellers. But be wary when they say they've corrected past problems; that doesn't guarantee new problems won't happen, says Mooney.

5. *Leaky roofs.* Stains within a home may indicate water problems. Even a new roof won't guarantee that a problem was totally resolved. "An owner may have added another layer of shingles on top of an existing leaky roof. The problem also may be due to inferior flashing," Mooney says. Buyers should ask how a problem was fixed and who did the work.

6. *Ineffective windows.* Windows that can't be opened and closed are problematic and should be serviced, repaired, or replaced. Windows that fog up may need maintenance or repair because they leak. The problem may be the result of poor installation which Mooney calls "a major epidemic." Steward says double-glazed windows that fog up due to faulty seals may look unattractive, but it's rarely cost effective to replace them if energy savings are the only goal.

7. *Damp facades.* Stains on wood siding may reveal entrapped moisture; cracks around bricks may indicate missing mortar. Know that hairline cracks around bricks may be OK, but in climates where freezing takes place, it's advisable to seal the cracks to reduce the possibility of freeze/thaw action causing spalling, or deterioration of the brick's face.

8. *Pesky pests.* Termites and carpenter ants may reside in a home and dine without being invited. They also leave few signs, except some mud tubes and sawdust, known as frass. Best rule: Quiz homeowners about prior unwanted pests and what they did to cure problems.

9. *Sagging wood floors.* Like foundation cracks, variations in wood floors are normal since wood is not a perfect material. Not acceptable: excessive slopes or a floor that feels like a trampoline when walked on. A marble is the simplest device for checking a wood floor. Place the marble on the floor. If it rolls away quickly, call an expert.

10. *Rot.* Most wood that's not treated is often vulnerable to moisture and fungal growth. Red flags are decay that appears brown and crumbly, breaks into cubes, or is soft. Pay attention to wood that touches dirt since it's more susceptible to picking up moisture and decay and allows an easy pathway for insects such as termites. Watch masonry or joints that are slow to dry.

If seller clients are required to make repairs before a closing, advise them to get three recommendations and bids before proceeding. If work was previously done, tell buyer clients to check permits to ensure the work was performed in compliance with local regulations.

Sources: H. Alan Mooney, Criterium Engineers, Portland, Maine; Diane Saatchi, The Corcoran Group, East Hampton, N.Y.; and Dan Steward, Pillar to Post, Tampa, Fla.

 *10 Signs There May Be Fraud*

The Federal Bureau of Investigation reports that mortgage fraud cases increased by 69 percent between 2003 and the second quarter of 2006. In its white paper, "The Detection, Investigation, and Deterrence of Mortgage Loan Fraud Involving Third Parties," the Federal

Financial Institutions Examination Council of Arlington, Virginia, suggests these red flags as indicators that fraud may be taking place.

- Cash is paid to the seller outside of the escrow arrangement.
- Cash is paid to the borrower in a purchase transaction.
- No money is due from the buyer at closing.
- A difference exists between the sale price on the HUD-1 form and the price on the sales contract.
- Related parties are involved in the transaction.
- The buyer must use a specific lender.
- Funds are paid to undisclosed third parties, indicating that there may be potential obligations.
- The sales price is changed to fit the appraisal.
- The sale is subject to the seller acquiring title.
- The loan is based on a buyer's stated income instead of a documented source.

5 Ways to Practice Law Unlawfully

1. Changing the wording in a purchase contract except for the sections designed to be filled in by a real estate licensee. Even if it's only a few words, don't mess with the preprinted portions of a contract form unless permitted to do so by your state's law.
2. Explaining to your client the meaning of a clause in the contract. Resist the temptation and refer the client to an attorney.
3. Telling a client "not to worry" about a clause in the contract since the seller will not try to enforce it.
4. Signing a document on behalf of your client, even with the client's approval, unless you have power of attorney.

5. Writing an addendum to the purchase contract. It's far less risky to include common contingencies as standard clauses and then cross them out if they don't apply.

Compiled by REALTOR® Magazine's editorial staff.

Avoid These 5 Contract Pitfalls

1. *Vaguely worded contingency clauses.* It's a rare contract that doesn't contain some contingencies, but be sure the clauses you include are specific about the time frames in which the parties must meet the contingency. The contract should also specify what options will be open to the parties if an inspection turns up a defect in the property.

2. *Failing to describe accurately the personal property* included in sale. Don't just write "per the MLS listing." To avoid disputes, list all items specifically.

3. *Too small a deposit.* Try to get a larger amount to ensure that the buyer is serious.

4. *Neglecting to document all agreements.* Be sure that oral agreements are reflected in the contract itself or in addenda drafted by an attorney and signed by the parties.

5. *Failing to disclose all material facts* relating to the sale. Surprises can sour a deal.

Sources: About.com and *The Real Estate Solutions Guide 2005,* published by *Florida REALTOR®* magazine.

🏠 *10 Ways to Lose Your License*

Thousands of real estate professionals lose their license every year—some through dishonest dealings, others through incompetence, and still others as the victims of circumstance. Your license is your lifeblood in this business. Keep it safe by avoiding these 10 mistakes.

1. *Playing with other people's money.* Money mistakes—sloppy bookkeeping, fund shuffling, borrowing clients' funds—represent the fastest ways to lose your license. Bill Titter, a former enforcement officer for the Texas Real Estate Commission, recalls a broker who agreed to hold $18,479 until closing so the buyer wouldn't spend it. The broker cashed the buyer's check and put the money in his own safety deposit box, then deducted expenses related to the deal without the buyer's knowledge. The broker's license was revoked. "If the money isn't yours, put it in escrow or in a trust account," says Titter.

2. *Misrepresentation.* Embellishing, obfuscating, omitting, or just plain fibbing: Don't do it. Misrepresentation and failure to disclose are the most common causes of lawsuits against licensees, says NATIONAL ASSOCIATION OF REALTORS® General Counsel Laurie Janik. Those lawsuits most often relate to inaccurate disclosure or nondisclosure of property condition. Know your state law, but no matter where you live, follow this simple rule: "When in doubt, disclose, and do it in writing," says William Moran, assistant commissioner of enforcement for the California Department of Real Estate.

3. *Mortgage fraud.* Say the buyers are short of cash for the down payment, and the salesperson arranges for them to borrow a little extra by fudging appraisal figures. It may seem like an innocent fix, but it's illegal to trick a lender into lending too much money against an overvalued property. Even if you don't lose your license in such a scheme, you can jeopardize your livelihood, according to Jon Goodman, a Colorado real estate attorney with Frascona, Joiner, Goodman and Greenstein PC. The U.S. Department of Housing and Urban Development is known to stop dealing with licensees simply because they were implicated in mortgage fraud, Goodman says.

4. *Criminal conviction.* Being a convicted criminal may affect your ability to obtain or keep a real estate license, depending on the crime and the state in which you work. In Texas, for example, felony crimes, such as rape, murder, and robbery, for which a person has been convicted or pled guilty to, can result in a license revocation, according to the Texas Real Estate Commission. A more common conviction, driving under the influence of alcohol or drugs, probably would not. In Arizona, the Department of Real Estate may give someone convicted of DUI a provisional license, but would require another licensed broker to sponsor the licensee and report on the person's sobriety. Provisional licenses are determined on an individual basis, depending on such factors as level of intoxication, how long ago the incident occurred, and whether the person has participated in a rehab program.

5. *Not cooperating with investigators.* If your real estate commission questions you, don't stonewall. "When licensees won't talk to us or provide us with records we've requested, that's a failure to cooperate with the investigation," says Whitney Clark, senior attorney with the New York department of state. "Usually, it's a sign they've done something wrong."

6. *Incompetence.* This category is a catchall of professional screwups. "We look for a pattern of conduct or a single act

that's so serious it demonstrates that the licensee lacks professional competence," says New York's Clark. A typical example: A property manager forgets to make tax or mortgage payments for an owner.

7. *Forgetting who hired you.* Undisclosed dual agency is a particular problem in states where buyer's agents are uncommon. "Listing brokers can get too close to the buyer and become a de facto dual agent," explains Al Jurczynski, New York's deputy secretary of state for business and licensing services. "In such cases, licensees forget whose interests they're supposed to be looking out for."

8. *Acting like a lawyer.* In some states, drafting or significantly altering sales contracts may constitute the unauthorized practice of law. But it's not always clear to brokers how far they can go. New York, for example, allows brokers to prepare simple purchase and lease contracts—not complex contracts. But what's the gauge for complexity? "We never see a simple contract," says New York's Clark. "Assume all contracts are complex." The conservative thing to do is to consult an attorney whenever an issue comes up that's outside the language of the form contract. The other risk of drafting a contract yourself is that you may do it wrong. In Oregon, Real Estate Commissioner Scott Taylor says he regularly sees contracts in which either the practitioners didn't say what was intended or the grammar was so poor it was impossible to determine the intent. The most typical mistakes occur when practitioners leave blanks because they're in a hurry, says Taylor.

9. *Not meeting license requirements.* It's the silliest reason to lose a license and the easiest to avoid. According to Titter, two or three Texas licensees each month forget to pay their renewal fees, and a few more fail to complete their continuing education requirements. Although salespeople should be responsible for staying on top of licensing requirements, supervising brokers need a system in place to make sure their licensees know and follow through on what's required. Brokers who let associates' licenses or education lapse risk disciplinary action or even a civil lawsuit.

10. *Letting salespeople run rampant.* Brokers must remember they have a duty to supervise the actions of all of their salespeople. Often it's not incompetence but inexperience that gets a salesperson in trouble—something that might have been avoided if the broker had only been paying closer attention. A supervising broker has a great responsibility, says California's Moran. "Too often, brokers don't take this responsibility seriously, and the public suffers."

Source: NAR's Legal Action Committee.

Ad Language: Keep It Fair

As a rule of thumb, property ads and promotions should focus on describing the property, not the sellers or potential buyers. Here are some fair housing guidelines from the U.S. Department of Housing and Urban Development on acceptable and unacceptable advertising phrases.

Race, Color, and National Origin

Unacceptable: Wording that describes the housing, the current or potential residents, or the neighborhood in racial or ethnic terms (e.g., traditional Irish neighborhood).

Acceptable: Racially neutral terms (rare find, desirable neighborhood).

Religion

Unacceptable: Ads with blatant phrases (no Jews, Christian home) and ads that use the legal name of an entity containing a religious reference (Roselawn Catholic Home, or a religious symbol such as a cross).

Acceptable: Secular terms such as Season's Greetings.

Sex

Unacceptable: Ads that indicate a gender preference (females only apply).

Acceptable: Commonly used physical descriptions of housing units; terms that aren't preferential or limiting (mother-in-law suite, bachelor apartment).

Handicap

Unacceptable: Ads that disallow handicap accessories (no wheelchairs).

Acceptable: Phrases that describe a property's features, services, facilities, or neighborhood (great view, fourth-floor walk-up, walk-in closets, jogging trails, walking distance to bus stop).

Familial Status

Unacceptable: Ads that limit the number or ages of children allowed or express a preference for adults, couples, or singles. (Fair housing law includes an exemption for housing designed specifically for older persons; learn more at www.hud.gov.)

Acceptable: Descriptions of properties, their services, facilities (or lack thereof), or neighborhoods (two-bedroom, cozy family room, no bicycles allowed, quiet streets).

Source: Adapted from the NATIONAL ASSOCIATION OF REALTORS®' *Real Estate Brokerage Essentials: Managing Legal and Business Issues,* 3rd ed.

3 Ways to Respond to Buyer Questions That Challenge Fair Housing Law

Problem: You've heard it a hundred times from buyers, and you still don't have a good answer: "What kinds of people live in this neighborhood?"

Solution: The key is to provide concrete information that'll give buyers a sense of the area without mentioning protected classes: race, color, religion, sex, national origin, handicap, or familial status. Next time, instead of stammering when a buyer poses this dreaded question, try these legal—yet customer-friendly—responses.

1. Focus on economic status and occupation, which aren't protected by fair housing law. If you mention people you know or have worked with in the area, don't describe them in a way that includes a protected class.

   Say: "This is a middle-income neighborhood. Many of the folks who live here work at the businesses downtown. It's a very easy commute from here. For example, Bob Smith, my accountant, lives in the next block."

2. Focus on specifics about the neighborhood that give a sense of its personality, such as whether it has many long-term residents or first-time home buyers. Information on the

number of sales in the area may also give buyers a sense of an area's stability and vitality.

Say: "Most of the houses in the subdivision were built about 20 years ago, and a lot of the original buyers still live here. Aren't the houses beautifully maintained?"

3. Focus on providing objective data from third-party sources. Making the data available to all clients also could protect you from charges of discrimination.

   Say: "I get that question a lot, so I asked the chamber of commerce to provide me with a fact sheet about the area's demographics that I could offer to all my clients. That way, you'll have all the data to take with you. I also put the chamber's number at the bottom so you can call if you have any more questions."

Compiled by REALTOR® Magazine's editorial staff.

9 Need-To-Know Federal Job Laws

If you hire for your brokerage, you're likely to be familiar with Title VII of the Civil Rights Act. That's the federal law that prohibits job discrimination on the basis of race, color, religion, sex, or national origin. But did you know there are more than a dozen federal laws that affect your employment practices, even if you have only one employee? Here are nine laws to keep on your radar screen. (Unless otherwise indicated, the laws apply to companies with a minimum of one employee.)

1. *Consumer Credit Protection Act.* The 1968 law protects employees from discharge because their wages have been garnished for debt and limits the amount of an employee's earnings that may be garnished in any one week.

2. *Electronic Communications Privacy Act.* Enacted in 1986, it sets out provisions for access, use, disclosure, and interception of, and privacy protections for, electronic communications. It also prohibits unlawful access to and certain disclosures of the contents of employee communications.

3. *Equal Pay Act.* This law, passed in 1963, prohibits sex-based wage discrimination between men and women in the same establishment who are performing under similar working conditions.

4. *Federal Unemployment Tax Act.* This 1939 law provides for unemployment compensation to workers who've lost their jobs. Most employers pay both a federal and a state unemployment tax.

5. *Occupational Safety and Health Act.* Enacted in 1970, the law imposes a general duty on employers to furnish a place of employment that's free from recognized hazards that are causing or are likely to cause death or serious physical harm to employees.

6. *Personal Responsibility and Work Opportunity Reconciliation Act.* Under this 1996 law, employers must report new hires to state welfare agencies so that the agencies in turn can report to the National Directory of New Hires that people who were on welfare got jobs. The law also addresses procedures for withholding child support from wages.

7. *Americans with Disabilities Act.* Enacted in 1990, the law prohibits discrimination in employment practices, including job application procedures, hiring, firing, advancement, compensation, and training. It applies to recruitment, advertising, tenure, layoff, leave, and fringe benefits, among others. Minimum company size: 15 employees.

8. *Age Discrimination in Employment Act.* This law, enacted in 1967, prohibits employment discrimination against persons 40 years of age or older. Minimum company size: 20 employees.

9. *Older Workers Benefit Protection Act.* Enacted in 1990, the law protects older workers from discrimination by employers based on age when providing employee severance and other benefits. Minimum company size: 20 employees.

Compiled by REALTOR® Magazine's editorial staff.

10 Transaction Documents You Must Keep

It's tempting once closing is over to dump the mountain of paper that every real estate transaction seems to generate. But clean out judiciously. You'll want to keep:

1. *The listing agreement.* To prove you were the exclusive representative of your client in case of a dispute.

2. *The signed or acknowledged agency disclosure form.* To protect yourself in case any questions of fiduciary responsibility or liability arise.

3. *The comparative market analysis.* To demonstrate how you and the seller arrived at a sale price.

4. *All marketing materials, including newspaper ads and printouts of online listings.* To protect yourself from charges of violating fair housing laws.

5. *All correspondence and phone logs with buyers, sellers, or other parties to the transactions.* To provide evidence of fact in case

of a charge of misrepresentation, which can be filed several years after the events occur.

6. *Inspection reports and copies of all invoices for repair work required before the sale*. To demonstrate what physical defects came to light during inspection and what repairs were done.

7. *The lead-based paint and other hazardous material disclosure forms, if applicable*. To ensure you have proof of compliance, keep lead paint forms for three years.

8. *A copy of the purchase contract and addenda*. To provide a record of the exact terms of the deal.

9. *A copy of the settlement statement (HUD-1 form)*. To keep a record of sellers' and buyers' transaction costs and to gain points with clients by sending a copy to them at tax time with an explanation prepared by your accountant of what they can deduct.

10. *Escrow account records relating to the transaction*. To prove the monies were managed and disbursed.

Adapted from REALTOR® Magazine Online's (REALTOR.org/realtormag) Risk Management section.

8 1031 Exchange Rules You Can't Ignore

These tax-deferred exchanges are great ways to postpone capital gains taxes on you or your clients' real estate investments. But be sure you follow the rules.

1. Exchanges can be used only for investment properties or properties owned for use in a business. They can't be used

for principal residences or for second homes unless that second property is used to generate rental income.

2. Exchanges must be for like-kind properties. The like-kind properties must both be used for investment or business purposes, but that doesn't mean they have to have the same exact use. An apartment can be exchanged for a strip mall, for example.

3. To meet the Internal Revenue Service guidelines for an exchange, you must identify the replacement property for the one you exchange within 45 days of the initial property transfer date. You may identify up to three properties of like value or as many properties as necessary to total the fair market value of the property you are exchanging.

Properties may also be exchanged for tenant-in-common interest shares in larger, institutional-grade property. Say your client owns a $1 million retail property. The client can exchange it for a 10 percent ownership interest in a $10 million property. There are a host of benefits to these fractional interest exchanges. Your investor clients may be able to buy into properties of a size and quality they couldn't otherwise afford. There's also the chance to trade their management responsibilities for ownership interests in a professionally managed property. The Securities and Exchange Commission and the NATIONAL ASSOCIATION OF REALTORS® are working together to find ways for real estate practitioners to be compensated in tenant-in-common transactions.

4. You must close on the replacement property within 180 days from the initial transfer date of your property to the other party. Note that IRS regulations now let you buy the replacement property first in what is called a reverse exchange. A reverse exchange must also be completed within 180 days.

5. If the property exchange isn't simultaneous, you must use a qualified intermediary—often a bank or an attorney—to hold the money until the other part of the exchange is complete.

6. If you end up with cash to even out the value of the two exchanged properties—often called a "boot"—that cash is taxable at current capital-gains rates.

7. All exchanged properties must be located in the United States.

8. If the property you receive in exchange is from a person related to you and you then sell the property within two years, the original exchange won't qualify for deferred capital gains.

Note: Like-kind exchanges are often complicated. A failure to follow the rules could mean the tax benefits of the exchange (the deferral of taxes on capital gains) are lost. Check with an attorney or other investment professional.

Compiled by REALTOR® Magazine's editorial staff.

6 Provisions Every Buyer's Agreement Should Have

1. The term of the agreement and the duties and responsibilities of the buyers' agent.

2. The fee buyers will pay their agent if they purchase a home during the term of the agreement, and whether the fee will be offset by any amounts paid to their agent by the seller or listing agent. The agreement should also disclose instances in which a seller or listing broker won't compensate a buyers' agent.

You may also want to consider including a retainer or hourly fee compensation clause in the buyer's agreement that states the buyer agent will be paid a fee or commission whether or not a customer purchases a home.

3. The circumstances under which buyers aren't obligated to pay a commission. With an exclusive right of representation agreement, buyers owe a commission on any property purchased during the time the contract is in force. Under an exclusive agency agreement, buyers have the flexibility to purchase properties they identify on their own but will still owe a commission if a purchased property is identified with the assistance of their agent. New construction and FSBO are the types of property that buyers are most likely to find themselves.

4. Procedures that will be followed if the agent shows the same property to more than one buyer or writes more than one contract on the same property. One option is to withdraw from representing one of the buyers. Another choice is to disclose the situation to both parties and obtain their written consent. This will create a dual agency relationship, however.

5. If the buyer's agent's company also accepts listings from sellers, provisions addressing the possible dual agency that may arise if the buyer becomes interested in a property listed with the company. Such provisions might provide for the buyer's consent to the disclosed dual agency, "designated agency" (where permitted by law), or arrangements for the buyer to seek other representation in that circumstance.

6. If "limited-service" or "MLS-only" listings are common in your marketplace, consider provisions addressing whether the buyer's agent will provide other services (including those ordinarily performed by a listing agent) to assist a buyer seeking to purchase such a listing and the additional compensation, if any, due from the buyer for such services.

Source: Lynn Madison, REBAC instructor, Lynn Madison Seminars (www.lynn madison.com), Palatine, Ill.

12 Ways to Be Sure You're Safe

1. Don't meet a prospect at a property. Insist that a prospect come to your office first.

2. Get identification. Get personal information on a prospect— a copy of the prospect's driver's license, a car description, and license plate number—before you go out on a showing. It's also a good idea to introduce the prospect to others in your office so that they can visually identify the person if needed. For sellers, check county property listings before you make a listing call.

3. Set up an emergency code word to alert your office that you need assistance. Choose a word that fits into a business discussion so that you don't alert your possible attacker.

4. Use your own car for showings. An assailant might have a weapon or an accomplice in his vehicle.

5. Plan for an escape route. Check out the house before a showing or open house so that you know where all the exits are.

6. Call in during and after a showing and at regular intervals during an open house. If you don't check in, your office will know you're in trouble.

7. Don't include your home address on your business cards, even if you work from home. It could be an invitation to a stalker.

8. Park where you can get out quickly. Don't let the prospect pull into a driveway behind you.

9. Don't drive where an assailant tells you to. Stay on streets with heavy traffic. When you can, pull close to another car on the right so the passenger door won't open. Then slam

on the brakes and get out of the car fast. Or crash your car into a signpost or a tree.

10. Walk behind your clients so you can't be surprised by an attack.

11. Take the offensive. If no weapon is present, deter your attacker by screaming and pushing him away. Keep your keys—with a pepper spray attached—in your hand at all times.

12. Trust your instincts. If you feel unsafe, leave. Your life is worth more than any commission.

Source: Washington Association of REALTORS® (www.warealtor.com).

Chapter 5

PERSONAL GROWTH

What Would Miss Manners Do?

"**Y**our packaging is the equivalent of curb appeal," says Marjorie Brody, president of Brody Communications Ltd., a Jenkintown, Pennsylvania, company that offers business communications and etiquette training. Just as consumers won't fall for a house that looks nice on the outside but is a dump on the inside, they won't fall for a salesperson who's well dressed but isn't gracious and respectful.

"Your professionalism sells and builds relationships," says Brody, "so you need to treat people so that they'll enjoy working with you, they'll trust you, and they'll ultimately refer you."

People have long bemoaned the death of professional service, which is why it's more important than ever to provide it, says Peter Post, director of the Emily Post Institute in Burlington, Vermont, which offers personal and professional etiquette and manners advice. "The capabilities you bring as a practitioner are really important, but ultimately consumers make the decision to work with you based on your personal skills," he says. "Real estate practitioners often forget that."

Post says the biggest nonprofessional behavior that limits

people is not thinking before they act and then doing or saying things they wish they hadn't. "If I had a single goal for the people I teach during one-day seminars, it would be to convince them to think before they act," he says.

What do you do when your mouth opens before your brain engages? Both Post and Brody recommend owning up. "Acknowledge and take responsibility for the situation," they advise. "Say you're sorry: 'I understand I was out of line, and I apologize.'"

"Second, have a solution," says Post. "Fixing a problem is especially important in the workplace," he explains. If you solve the problem you've created, you'll set yourself apart.

"People are so self-absorbed and busy that they lose sight of the fact that how you treat others—sending a thank-you note, referring business to them—differentiates you," says Brody. "It's another piece of what sets you apart."

Here are other ways—from courtesy to memory power to volunteering—to put your best self forward.

Professional Courtesy: 30 Ways to Show It Every Day

Real estate is a reputation business. Bolster your reputation by showing respect for the public, the properties you show, and your peers.

Respect for the Public

1. Always follow the Golden Rule. (Do unto others as you would have them do to you.)

2. Respond promptly to inquiries and requests for information.

3. Schedule appointments and property showings as far in advance as possible; call if you're delayed or must cancel an appointment.

4. When showing an occupied home, always ring the doorbell or knock. If there's no answer, announce yourself loudly before entering. Do the same before entering any closed room.

5. Anticipate unexpected situations, such as enthusiastic pets, at listings so that you can act quickly and appropriately when you're with buyers.

6. Present a professional appearance at all times. Dress appropriately and drive a clean car.

7. Be aware of and meet all deadlines.

8. Promise only what you can deliver—and keep your promises.

9. Don't tell people what you think. Tell them what you know.

10. Leave your business card at showings if you're not prohibited from doing so by local rules.

11. Never criticize property in the presence of the owner.

12. If sellers are home during a showing, ask their permission before using the telephone or bathroom.

13. Advise other brokers' clients to direct questions to their agent.

14. Communicate clearly; avoid jargon.

15. Be aware of and respect cultural differences.

Respect for Property

16. Be responsible for everyone you allow to enter listed property.

17. Never allow unaccompanied access to property without permission.

18. Enter property only with permission, even if you have a lockbox key or combination.

19. When the occupant is absent, leave the property as you found it (lights, heating, cooling, drapes, and so on). If you think something is amiss (for example, you see signs of vandalism), contact the listing broker immediately.

20. Don't allow anyone to eat, drink, smoke, dispose of trash, use bathing or sleeping facilities, or bring pets. Leave the house as you found it unless instructed otherwise.

21. Use sidewalks and walkways. If the weather is bad, take off shoes and boots at the entranceway before showing the property.

22. Make sure heating and cooling controls are set correctly in vacant properties, and check the outside of the property for damage or vandalism.

Respect for Peers

23. Identify your REALTOR® and professional status in all contacts with other REALTORS®.

24. Be aware that large electronic files with attachments or lengthy faxes may be a burden on recipients.

25. When showing a property, notify the listing broker if there appears to be inaccurate information on the listing.

26. If you're the listing agent, share important information about the property, including the presence of pets, secu-

rity systems, and whether sellers will be present during showings.

27. Avoid the inappropriate use of endearments or other denigrating language.

28. Don't prospect at other practitioners' open houses or similar events.

29. After a showing, call the listing broker to report the results.

30. Alert the listing broker if anything appears wrong with the property.

Source: Adapted from the NATIONAL ASSOCIATION OF REALTORS®' "Pathways to Professionalism," which was developed by the NAR Professional Standards Committee. This list of voluntary courtesies is not all-inclusive and may be supplemented by local custom and practice.

5 Ways to Make People Happy

Your business success depends on how well you build positive relationships with customers. If you can make them happy, you'll keep them coming back.

1. *Be honest.* Many people have been conditioned to expect an evasive or equivocal response from companies. If customers ask how your service differs from that of competitors, give an honest and straightforward answer.

2. *Let them talk.* People enjoy talking about themselves; your customers are no exception. Ask questions not just about their real estate goals, but about their family, profession, and hobbies. Pay attention to how much of the time you talk compared with the time your customer talks. If you

find that you're talking too much, make an effort to ask more questions and listen.

3. *Show you care.* Thoughtful acts say a great deal about who you are. Record the names of customers' children, pets, or birthdays and use the information when asking how their family is doing or to send a card. E-mail them a news article about their favorite band or send a recipe you think they'd like.

4. *Be persistent (but not aggressive).* Do you know whether your customers think your actions are aggressive? If they perceive you as being too pushy, they may back away from doing business with you. Rather than guess, simply ask them how often they want you to contact them and what time of the day they'd like to be reached.

5. *Don't break your word.* If you tell customers that you'll e-mail them the next morning with a new batch of home listings, follow through. If you say that you'll always return their call within an hour, do it. People never forget a broken promise.

Source: Jerry Acuff, *The Relationship Edge in Business: Connecting with Customers and Colleagues When It Counts* (John Wiley & Sons, 2004). Adapted with permission of John Wiley & Sons, Inc.

How to Improve Civility in the Profession

Although the real estate business is extremely competitive, practicing niceties not only improves your professionalism, it also elevates the industry. Practice these common courtesies:

- Say please, thank you, I'm sorry, and excuse me.
- Make a positive difference by saying a kind word or offering your assistance.

- Share information.

- Pick up trash around the property, even if it's not your listing.

- Say hello to the neighbors.

- Extend good wishes to colleagues; celebrate their successes.

- Reach out to those in need; give back to your community.

- Do one thing every day to wow someone or brighten someone's day.

- Show gratitude in your life—it makes a difference in your attitude.

Source: Susan Fignar, Pur-sue Inc. (www.pur-sue.com), Itasca, Ill.

10 Timely Tech Etiquette Tips

Without a little sensitivity, a reliance on technology can get in the way of good old-fashioned manners. Here are good habits to keep in mind.

1. *Advise and get consent.* Expecting an urgent message via phone, e-mail, or instant message when meeting with clients or peers? Advise them at the outset so that the temporary distraction won't be taken as an insult.

2. *Update outgoing messages.* When you know you'll be unavailable, update your e-mail auto-response and voice mail message letting people know how long you expect to be tied up and when you expect to be able to respond.

3. *Ask before clicking.* As a courtesy, ask homeowners' permission before taking photos of their house, and explain how the photos will be used.

4. *Some things are better discussed in person or over a landline.* Have discussions about personal or financial information face to face or over a landline. Cellular and cordless phone conversations can be easily overheard. Advise those on the other end why you're calling so that they can be discreet.

5. *Get to the point.* When you use e-mail or leave a voice mail message, don't waste words. With voice mail, clearly enunciate your name and the time and reason for the call, and repeat your phone number at the end.

6. *Confer before conferencing.* Advise participants of the agenda for a conference call and let them know who will attend. As the initiator, moderate the call, starting with introductions.

7. *Schedule faxing.* If there are scores of pages to the document, call ahead and see whether the receiving party would prefer you to send it after hours, when the transmission won't tie up the line.

8. *Get a Tablet.* Opening a notebook computer and typing away puts up a barrier between you and clients. If you must record notes on the fly, consider a Tablet PC, which includes a special pen for on-screen note taking. It's less intrusive and doesn't give up any of the convenience of your portable computer.

9. *Don't hog the Wi-Fi.* Hot spots in restaurants and coffee shops are a customer convenience, not a field office. If you can't complete a task in the time it takes to finish that latte or meal, move on to a public space like a library.

10. *Avoid spam, period.* No one wants it, no one appreciates it, and it always reflects poorly on the manners of the sender.

Source: Michael Antoniak, REALTOR® Magazine technology writer.

5 Surefire Conversation Starters

If you ever find yourself standing alone at events, here are five ways to get the conversation rolling.

1. *Have an introduction ready.* This seven- to nine-second opener should be pleasant and keyed to the event. Be ready, when asked what you do, to talk not about your job title but how your work benefits others.

2. *Pay attention to name tags.* Badges or name tags frequently contain information you can use in a conversation, such as company affiliations or hometowns.

3. *Talk about the venue.* Look around for an interesting aspect of your surroundings. Possible topics could be architectural elements, the decor, or the food.

4. *Wear something unusual.* An intriguing brooch, necklace, tie, or lapel pin is an invitation for others to approach you. Similarly, if you admire something somebody else is wearing, make a comment about it.

5. *Be informed.* Before the event, read a national, local, or trade publication so that you're aware of the latest headlines. Current events are great fodder for conversations, and you'll come across as being well-informed. Caveat: Avoid discussing controversial topics with strangers, at least until their opinions are known.

Source: Susan RoAne, principal of The RoAne Group (www.susanroane.com), San Francisco, and speaker and author of *How to Create Your Own Luck: The "You Never Know" Approach to Networking, Taking Chances, and Opening Yourself to Opportunity* (John Wiley & Sons, 2004) and *What Do I Say Next?: Talking Your Way to Business and Social Success* (Warner Books, 1999).

9 Tips for Dining with Style

Whether you're hosting an introductory meeting with referral customers or a client-appreciation event, follow these tips to dine with style.

1. *Make a reservation at a place you frequently patronize.* Or if you're trying out a new restaurant, be sure to test it ahead of time and get to know the staff so that you can address them by name.

2. *Find out about food allergies.* You need to be sensitive to any food allergies of your dining guests so that you can pick a restaurant accordingly and order shared dishes with finesse.

3. *Set the tone for what to order.* Your guests will take their cues from you if you offer a cocktail, recommend a good appetizer, or tell them the restaurant is known for its lobster dishes.

4. *Order manageable foods.* Poached pear in wine sauce, spaghetti, and peas are hard to eat. Order dishes that won't spill, drop, or take too much effort. Avoid anything that you know gets stuck in your teeth, is too crunchy, or contains a lot of garlic.

5. *Practice abstemious dining.* There's no quicker way to make a bad impression than by overeating or overdrinking.

6. *Turn off your cell phone.* If there's a call you absolutely have to take, tell your guests that you're expecting an important phone call in the next 30 minutes that you must take and that you'd do the same for them if it was their closing.

7. *Raise a toast.* Don't forget to acknowledge the purpose of the meal and show how much you appreciate the guests.

Whether it's "Here's to our ongoing working relationship" or "I wanted to thank you for the five referrals you sent me this year," raising a toast makes the guests feel special.

8. *There's no such thing as going Dutch.* If you want someone's business, you have to show some love. Always pick up the tab. And save those receipts; if you discuss business, a portion of the meal will be tax deductible.

9. *No check, please.* Don't have the check come to the table. Set up a house account at the restaurant or pay for the meal before or after.

Source: Maureen Costello, Image Launch (www.imagelaunch.com), Lake Forest, Ill.

7 Ways to Update Your Look

A successful real estate professional needs to look fresh and modern without being too trendy. Ask yourself these 10 questions to see if your look is helping you succeed or holding you back.

1. *Is your hair up-to-date?* If you look at a photo of yourself from 10 or 20 years ago and the only difference is a few wrinkles on your face, it may be time to freshen up your 'do.

2. *Do your clothes fit right?* Take a long, hard look at yourself in the mirror. Do your clothes fit the body you're living in now?

3. *Are you well-groomed from head to toe?* Your clothes should be clean, pressed, and lint-free. Both men and women should have their nails manicured and shoes polished.

4. *Are you modern, without being high-fashion?* Invest in good quality basics, such as nice wool pants and a cashmere sweater or a solid shirt and tie. Exude quality without being flashy.

5. *Are your accessories polished?* Your briefcase should be in good repair and not nicked up or look as if it's been dragged through mud. That also goes for your writing tablet portfolio. You should also have a good pen. It doesn't have to be a Montblanc, but it should be nice enough to convey that you're well prepared and ready to do business.

6. *Does your car say the right things about you?* Your car reflects on you as a professional. It should give you credibility without being ostentatious. Be sure to have it cleaned weekly.

7. *Do you mirror the people you want to work with?* If you want to work with corporate executives, dress like a corporate executive. If you want to target moneyed socialites in charity circles, dress like you belong there and participate by writing a check.

Source: Maureen Costello, Image Launch (www.imagelaunch.com), Lake Forest, Ill.

🏠 *7 Steps to Get Out of a Slump*

Even top salespeople go through slow periods. The difference is that they don't let a few lost sales get them down. Here are some suggestions on how to get back on track fast.

1. *Don't waste time feeling sorry for yourself.* Even if your slump is caused by factors you can't control, such as a downturn in the market or a family illness, your only option is to redouble your efforts, says Danielle Kennedy in *Selling the Danielle Kennedy Way* (Prentice Hall, 1991). If you now have

to make 100 calls instead of 50 to get 10 listings, then just start making the 100 calls.

2. *Get back in front of clients and the community.* Something as simple as delivering holiday dinners to the less fortunate or participating in a car wash to buy equipment for the local soccer team gives you a positive reason to contact prospects and old customers.

3. *Reevaluate your pricing and services compared with those of your competitors.* Reevaluation doesn't necessarily mean cutting your commission; instead, maybe you need to offer more sophisticated marketing plans or a password-protected portion of your web site where clients can follow the progress of their transaction.

4. *Branch out.* Send a letter offering consulting services to your clients on purchasing real estate investments or the payback they can reap from home improvements (use *Remodeling* Magazine's "Cost vs. Value Report" at wwwthings.remodeling.hw.net). Charge by the hour to bring in income.

5. *Get another perspective.* Even if you're experienced, you may have fallen into unconscious bad habits that are hurting your listing or sales conversion rate. An objective critique from a peer or your sales manager may help you see something you didn't even realize was a problem.

6. *Shun those with a negative view.* Being around a complainer or a whiner will bring you even further down.

7. *Analyze what works, and then do more of it.* Where is your current business coming from? Referrals? Sign calls? Track your business, and then concentrate more of your efforts on what you do best.

Source: Compiled by REALTOR® Magazine's editorial staff.

Tips for Volunteers

Community service gives you the chance to network and express yourself outside of work. Follow these simple tips to get more involved.

- Find an area of service that has personal meaning for you or someone you care about. You may be interested in working with the elderly, the poor, or children.

- Determine the amount of time you have to offer. Don't worry if you start out small. It's more important to be consistent and live up to your commitment.

- Volunteer for special one-time events, such as outings for seniors, hospital parties, or races.

- Investigate charities to make sure they spend only a small percentage of their donations on overhead.

- Look in your own backyard. Most state and many local REALTOR® associations have organized volunteer efforts that would welcome your support.

Adapted from REALTOR® Magazine Online's (REALTOR .org/realtormag) Good Neighbor and For Rookies sections.

5 Ways to Build Your Memory Power

Do you sometimes have trouble putting a name to a face? If so, here are five ideas for improving your memory. Try them now, before you forget!

1. *Slow down and listen.* A lot of people rush through information, rather than taking time on the front end to be clear on what they're trying to remember.

2. *Manage your stress level.* Stress is the No. 1 killer of memory. Just take a breath and tell yourself, "It will come to me."

3. *Think visually.* Pictures are the language of your memory. If something is really important to remember, try to tag it with a visual representation.

4. *Have a system.* You need a way to organize information in your mind. The system could be anything—mental file folders, word associations, visual associations, or storytelling. A story in *The Washington Post* detailed how former White House Chief of Staff Andrew Card employs a "mental kitchen": top-priority items are on the stove, long-range items are stored in the freezer, and so on.

5. *Use spaced repetition.* The difference between short-term and long-term memory is spaced repetition. If you review information an hour, a day, and a week after your initial exposure, you'll have improved recall.

Source: Eric Plantenberg and Roger Seip, co-owners, Freedom Speakers & Trainers (www.deliverfreedom.com), Madison, Wis.

6 Signs of Burnout

If any of these signs ring true for you, your workload may be causing job burnout.

1. *You wake up in the middle of the night* and start trying to solve a work-related problem.

2. *You frequently complete the sentences* of someone you're talking to.

3. *You regularly feel overwhelmed* with the amount of work you have to complete.

4. *You run late* all the time.

5. *You often find it hard to concentrate*, especially on more complicated tasks.

6. *You get angry easily*, often over minor things.

And 5 Ways to Curb It

1. *Have a plan of action* for each day, week, and month. Knowing what you want to achieve will help you focus and reduce the feeling that you're not accomplishing your goals.

2. *Concentrate on doing one thing at a time*. Trying to eat lunch, talk to a client, and put the finishing touches on a property ad due that day is a surefire recipe for stress and mistakes.

3. *Choose your battles wisely*. Don't make winning a must unless it's important.

4. *Know your limits*. Pushing yourself too hard leads to poor performance and mental fatigue.

5. *Get out more*. Walk around the block, exercise, or pamper yourself with a new tie or a manicure.

Source: REALTOR® Magazine Online's (REALTOR.org/realtormag) "Reducing Stress" Prepackaged Sales Meeting.

Quiz: How Balanced Is Your Life?

Assign the number that, for you, applies to each statement. Then total your numbers for a composite score that will reveal how well you're juggling life's demands.

Rarely (0), Sometimes (1), Frequently (2)

____ I say no to unrealistic requests from clients.

____ I say no to unrealistic requests from family.

____ I say no to unrealistic requests from my boss and colleagues.

____ I keep my commitment to exercise and healthy eating.

____ My family would say I give them my undivided attention and patiently listen to them.

____ My clients, boss, and colleagues would say I'm focused on what I do.

____ My doctor would say I watch my health, what I eat and drink, and how much I exercise.

____ I go to sleep at night feeling I haven't shortchanged my work, my family, or myself.

___ I feel more in control than out of control of my life.

___ I make changes in my life when I find I'm doing something wrong (like failing this quiz).

If You Scored

0–6. You're a ticking time bomb. Your life isn't just out of balance; it's out of control. You most likely won't do anything to put your life in balance until a crisis—a job or big client loss, illness, divorce, trouble with your kids, or drug or alcohol problems—hits. This quiz is a much less expensive and debilitating kick in the pants than those alternatives. Make some changes now!

7–15: You need to make tweaks, but you're on the right road. It's not easy to stay balanced in a world that conspires to throw you off track weekly, daily, and sometimes hourly. But you understand the need for and have taken steps toward prioritization. Don't take your balancing act for granted because you could easily slip into ticking time bomb territory.

16–20: Congratulations, you're winning at life! You're the envy of your colleagues, friends, and family. You're on track for a long and healthy life and, more important, one with few regrets. Enjoy the days, weeks, and years ahead.

Source: Dr. Mark Goulston, psychiatrist and author of three books, including *Get Out of Your Own Way at Work* (Putnam Adult, 2005).

Schedule Family Time

Problem: My spouse and kids get upset when I miss family dinners or when I have to forgo weekend plans for listings, showings, or closings. What can I do so that they're not disappointed and I don't lose business?

Solution: If you honestly believe you're going to lose business by putting your family first, you lack sufficient confidence in your professional ability to be a top salesperson. When you tell potential buyers and sellers you have a conflicting appointment—dinner with family is an appointment, as are children's recitals and soccer games—immediately offer up an alternative day and time. Most people want to do business with busy people since they consider them successful. They also understand people's allegiance to family.

No amount of money is worth missing family activities; you'll never recapture that lost time. To be sure you value family time as much as your business appointments, write dates on your paper calendar or enter them on your handheld device. If you occasionally must cancel family dates, have a heart-to-heart talk with loved ones to explain why.

A hypothetical explanation might be, "I know I promised to take you to the baseball game (dinner, park), but I have to break our date. We'll reschedule for next week. I appreciate your understanding. This is important to our family's well-being and could mean a longer vacation next summer."

Source: Nelson Zide, broker, ERA Key Realty Services, Framingham, Mass.

17 Ways to Add Balance to Your Life

Finding time for yourself, creating a happy home life, and succeeding at work aren't impossible if you learn to set limits, periodically say no, and forgo expectations of perfection in yourself and others. Real estate consultant and author Danielle Kennedy has learned to meet this challenge, with help from a flexible, involved spouse (a former real estate salesperson turned boat captain) and their eight children. Here are Kennedy's 17 top tips.

1. Prioritize by not saying yes to all requests and learning to say no kindly but firmly. Example: "I'd love to help you out, but I already have a commitment. Let's try again another time." People appreciate honesty and sincerity.

2. Eat well, exercise, and have regular checkups. You'll have more energy, jump-start your endorphins, and be happier.

3. Surround yourself with compassionate friends who understand your demands and won't criticize your juggling act.

4. Yield on expectations that require perfection of yourself, family, and colleagues. Example: The house needn't always be spotless; every project needn't be done perfectly, but try your best.

5. Delegate tasks among family and co-workers. For example: A six-year-old can make her bed; a nine-year-old can make his lunch; colleagues can cover for you when you go on vacation.

6. Cook a few meals in advance one day a week. Also prepare more servings than needed so that there are leftovers for another meal.

7. If you have kids, work for a company whose management values family. If you're the broker, make family values part of your company culture. Example: Don't schedule a sales meeting at 5 P.M. when parents need to pick up children.

8. If you can afford it, hire help around the house so that you have more time to spend with family and pursue favorite hobbies. Consider bringing on a babysitter, gardener, or cleaning service.

9. Share tasks with colleagues and friends. Organize car pools and cooperatives for babysitting and food shopping.

10. Schedule regular dates with yourself—quiet lunches, manicures—to smell the proverbial roses.

11. Find a new passion or revisit an old one. Bake, golf, or play bridge.

12. If you're part of a couple, have a weekly date to maintain romance.

13. Curtail spending by following a budget so that you don't need to work excessively to pay bills. Two-career couples shouldn't delude themselves that their combined checks allow them to spend more.

14. Get and stay organized, which sets a good example for colleagues and family members. Set up a home command post where you keep your keys, bills, and other important papers.

15. Keep routines going to maintain some normalcy even in the face of major snafus. Example: Continue driving the kids to their activities even if the kitchen remodel hits a snag and the contractor needs more of your time.

16. Keep family life enjoyable by sharing activities. Bowl with your children, have dinner together (without the TV on), choose a movie everyone wants to see. Don't let family life become boot camp.

17. Praise yourself, family, and colleagues. They'll return the favor.

Source: Danielle Kennedy, Danielle Kennedy Productions, Pacific Palisades, Calif., and author of *WorkingMoms.Calm: How Smart Women Balance Family & Career* (Thomson South-Western, 2002).

🏠 *10 Tips for Reducing Stress*

Stress can't be eliminated, but it can be managed. Try these remedies if you're going into overload.

1. *Get to know your stress triggers.* Inventory your activities for a week, noting the circumstances and people that cause you stress. Just knowing a situation causes you stress can reduce its impact.

2. *Learn to relax.* Practice meditation, stretching, or deep breathing. Or try progressive relaxation: Lie on your back and tighten each muscle area, then relax it, beginning with the face and ending with the toes. Another strategy: visualization. Imagine yourself in a quiet state, and you'll relax.

3. *Exercise regularly.* Set aside time at least twice a week for strenuous physical exercise. Exercise releases endorphins, stretches and relaxes muscles, and invigorates the mind and body.

4. *Stick to a healthy diet.* Eat the right things at regular intervals.

5. *Perform more difficult tasks when your energy level is at its peak.* Prospecting, with its rejections, is stressful, so get it out of the way first thing.

6. *Take minivacations.* Plan for downtime every day. Once in a while, call in "well" and take a day off to play.

7. *Abandon the 24/7 work week.* Ask clients not to call you after 7 P.M., except in emergencies. Then turn off your cell phone or BlackBerry in the evenings.

8. *Reclaim control of your thoughts and attitude.* Don't focus on the negative or worry about possible failures. For example,

if you're not completely prepared for a presentation, think of your past record of successes and tell yourself you're confident.

9. *Don't be too hard on yourself when you make a mistake or lose a sale.* Instead, try to analyze what happened and learn from your error.

10. *Look at the positive aspects of your job.* You're your own boss. You work long hours, but you can take off at 4 P.M. to coach your daughter's soccer team.

Sources: "Burnout: A Manager's Worst Nightmare," *Supervision* (National Research Bureau, Aug. 2001); REALTOR® Magazine Online's (REALTOR.org/realtormag) Broker and Reducing Stress Sales Meeting sections.

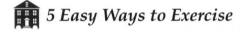 **5 Easy Ways to Exercise**

Studies reported in the *Journal of the American Medical Association* indicate that even 30 minutes a day of exercise has a big payoff. Here are strategies:

1. *Park three blocks from the home you're visiting and walk briskly the rest of the way.* Even short walks can increase your fitness level. And it's an easy way to preview the neighborhood.

2. *Do 10 minutes of stomach crunches and leg lifts before you get out of bed.* Increase the number daily until you reach at least 50 of each.

3. *Get two benefits for one.* Combine aerobic (stepper, treadmill) and strength (weights, rubber bands) into the same workout—doing 10 minutes of each and gradually working up to 30 minutes of each. It reduces monotony and gives your heart and your skeleton a workout.

4. *Get a dog.* The need to exercise the dog will give you a reason to walk. And studies have shown that spending time with a pet raises your levels of mood-enhancing chemicals.

5. *Count what you do.* Attach a pedometer to your belt during your daily activities. Set a steps-per-day goal. Walking one mile a day burns 3,500 calories a month, the equivalent of one pound.

Sources: "Exercise: What a Little Can Do," Sora Song, *Time* magazine, Sept. 22, 2003; Health & Fitness Tips (www.health-fitness-tips.com); and The President's Council on Physical Fitness and Sports (www.fitness.gov).

5 Weeks to Better Cash Flow

When you depend on commissions, cash flow can fall off at any time. To protect yourself, you need to put extra focus on winning the cash-flow war, says Fred Rewey, president of the American Cash Flow Association and author of *Winning the Cash Flow War* (John Wiley & Sons, 2005).

Week One

Know what you spend—and what you owe.

- *Make a list or a spreadsheet of all current monthly income sources, regular and recurring expenses, and outstanding debts.* A good model can be found at the Consumer Credit Counseling Services site, www.cccsintl.org.

- *Stop the "leakage."* Some people can spend up to 30 percent of their money in small purchases, says Rewey. Keep a log for one month to track expenses.

- *Level out your cash flow.* Resist the urge to increase either personal or business spending in a good year. Instead average your income over a number of years and use the average as a basis for budgeting.

Week Two

It's hard to stick to a total austerity program for long. Remember your last diet? But you can cut back and see positive results, says Rewey.

- *Downsize your discretionary spending.* Rent a video instead of going out to a movie, pick up nice quality takeout instead of going to a restaurant, and wash your own car, suggests Richard Jenkins, editor-in-chief of MSN Money.

- *Analyze your selling expenses, and eliminate those that don't pay off.* Determine the cost per lead for the advertising media you use. Code each advertising source, calculate the number of leads you receive from the source, then divide the number by the total expenditure. Focus your advertising efforts on those with the biggest payoff.

- *Reduce banking fees and surcharges.* Lower fees save you more than the small amount you earn on interest-bearing checking accounts. Also look for banks that offer low- or no-fee deals for special groups, such as those over 50 years old.

Week Three

Get out of the interest trap. Interest paid on debt, with the exception of home mortgages and some home-equity loans, is nondeductible and a total drain on your cash flow.

- *Assess which debts have the highest interest rates and repay them first.* According to Terry Savage, syndicated columnist and author of numerous books including *The Savage Truth on Money* (John Wiley & Sons, 2001), if you double the monthly minimum payment (and don't charge any more), you'll be out of debt in approximately three years.

- *Apply for credit cards with lower interest rates.* Check out www.creditcards.com for a comparison of card rates. Rewey suggests negotiating with credit-card companies to obtain a lower rate (your current credit-card company doesn't want to lose you) or transferring balances from high- to low-rate cards. Beware: Transferring balances can affect your credit rating if the cards are new. The transfer creates additional credit inquiries, which can lower a rating.

- *Roll debts into a home-equity loan.* You can deduct the interest payments for loans used to pay off debts. Deductions are limited to the lesser of $100,000 or the total fair market value of the home reduced by the total home acquisition, including sale price, points, and commission, and any grandfathered debt. *Note:* Grandfathered debt is defined as mortgage loans on your current home taken out before October 13, 1987. For more details, read IRS Publication 936, Home Mortgage Interest Deduction, available at www.irs.gov.

Week Four

Increase your income. It's the easiest way to save, especially if you can reduce your living expenses, too.

- *Prospect more.* Determine how many contacts it takes to make a sale; then be sure you make at least that many contacts each week.

- *Use your free time to earn a second income.* In the NATIONAL ASSOCIATION OF REALTORS®' *2005 Member Profile*, REALTORS® worked an average of 46 hours a week. An easy way to enhance income is to do something related to sales, such as appraisal or property management, suggests Rewey. Or act as a consultant on seller carryback financing. With this specialty (which may require a license in some states), you can use your real estate contacts to connect sellers with funders (private individuals or insurance companies that will purchase the loan for a lump sum) and pocket a referral fee on the sale.

- *Turn a hobby or skill into an income source.* If you antique, sell your finds on eBay. If you're great at home repairs, offer to help your all-thumbs neighbors.

Week Five

Save 10 percent of your earnings, more if you work on commission, says Rewey.

- *Compound.* Thanks to the miracle of compounding, a $3,000 annual investment in a Roth IRA, growing in the stock market tax-free at an historical average return of 10.6 percent, will net you more than $600,000 in 30 years.

- *Use automatic reinvestment plans.* Many stocks and mutual funds offer automatic deduction plans that take money from your checking account on a monthly basis and buy stock, which can then be deposited in your retirement account. Be sure to select the option to reinvest your dividends for added savings. You can also set up an automatic deduction for U.S. Savings Bonds.

Compiled by REALTOR® Magazine's editorial staff.

Chapter 6

PROFESSIONAL DEVELOPMENT

The Well-Trained Shall Inherit the Business

When the going gets tough, the tough get going.

That's never been more true for real estate professionals. Many markets have tightened, intensifying the competition for getting and selling listings. Now's the time to take advantage of every resource you can to fortify your skills.

"I'm telling our clients today that this is their time," says Mike Ferry of The Mike Ferry Organization, a real estate training company in Irvine, California, and Richmond, Virginia. "The need for salespeople who are well-trained and have good skills is at its highest right now." Ferry says he's coaching 4,500 practitioners, "and their business is way up because they know what to do."

Danielle Kennedy, a trainer at Danielle Kennedy Productions in Pacific Palisades, California, agrees salespeople must be stronger than ever. "You need to grow constantly because this business is about constant change, and you must stay on top of those changes so that you can interpret for consumers what's going on in the transaction or in a market."

Besides interpretation, consumers want three things from you, Kennedy says. First is knowledge. "You'd better be on top of things like inventory, community amenities, and finance," she says. Second is speed. "Consumers don't have a lot of patience today, so you have to stay educated on ways to complete aspects of the transaction as quickly as possible." Third, consumers want trust. "They want the intimacy of being able to say, 'I trust you and don't want to do business with anybody but you.' When you build trust, you're on the road to generating a lifetime of referrals."

"All of this takes [an investment in] professional development," says Kennedy. "Your awareness has to expand, and it expands only through education."

Here's more on leveraging professional development into long-term career success.

3 Alternative Paths

Your real estate experience can be the door to many career options.

Coach/Trainer/Speaker

Sometimes, [because of the constant travel], you can't remember what city you're in, but there's a real thrill when someone gets it, knowing that you may have changed a life.

—*Joe Meyer, Joe Meyer Presentations Inc.*
(www.joemeyer.com), Lake Grove, New York

Skill Set   Public speaking ability, subject matter knowledge and experience, educational orientation, empathy.

Training Needed   Presentation skills, constant updates on industry trends. Designation available through the Real Estate Educators Association. International Coach Federation accredits training programs for coaches.

Earning Potential   Sixty-five percent of National Speakers Association members earned $1,000–$5,000 for a training session and 45 percent earned $2,000–$5,000 for a keynote presentation, according to the organization's "2005 Member Demographic Survey."

Pluses   Good earning potential. Chance to share knowledge with others. Can be pursued part-time—about 29 percent of respondents to NSA's survey characterize themselves as independent, part-timers. And nearly 28 percent of respondents said they held fewer than 20 speaking engagements in a year.

Minuses   Constant travel. Irregular income. The frustration of knowing some students don't grasp what you're teaching.

Sources: Mike Ferry, The Mike Ferry Organization (www.mikeferry.com), Irvine, Calif.; ICF 2003 Survey, International Coach Federation (www.coach federation.org), Lexington, Ky.; Joe Meyer; Real Estate Educators Association (www.reea.org), Mt. Royal, N.J.; National Speakers Association (nsaspeaker.org), Tempe, Ariz.; and Richard Zackon, International Coach Federation.

Relocation Specialist

I figured out that my wiring was geared more to a Monday-through-Friday environment than to sales. In relocation, no two days are the same. I work with brokers, national and international corporations, and third-party relocation companies. Moving is one of the biggest stressors behind divorce and death, so the job lets me really help transferees by matching them with the best agent for them. It's also a great profession to see what other real estate companies are doing and to learn what's happening in other markets that might impact ours.

—*Sherrie Jones-Porter, vice president of relocation,*
Esslinger-Wooten-Maxwell Inc., REALTORS®, Miami

Skill Set   Strong customer service and communication skills, ability to work under pressure, patience and diplomacy, budgeting skills.

Training Needed   Understanding of the corporate relocation process, extensive knowledge of the community, languages if dealing with international transferees.

Earning Potential   Compensation can run from around $30,000 plus bonuses to six figures for a top job at a large brokerage company or corporation, according to Chicago-based relocation network Leading Real Estate Companies of the World.

Pluses   Structured office environment. No need to close. Stable salary base plus commission. Lots of variety—every deal is different.

Minuses   Limited face-to-face client contact. Paperwork. Need to deal with more inflexible corporate organizations. Must balance needs of customers and sales associates. Resentment from sales associates over referral fees charged.

Sources: Ernie Brescia, Century 21 Real Estate Corp., Parsippany, N.J.; Employee Relocation Council (www.erc.org), Washington, D.C.; Long & Foster Relocation, Fairfax, Va.; Pamela O'Connor, Leading Real Estate Companies of the World (www.leadingre.com), Chicago; Petey Parker (www.peteyparker.com); Kim Quinlan, Keller Williams Houston Memorial; and Barbe Ratcliffe, formerly with Weichert Relocation, Morris Plains, N.J.

Mortgage Broker/Banker

Although I do miss the strong personal relationships I formed with my sales clients, I like the analytical nature of mortgage brokerage. Either the figures are there to do the deal or they aren't.

—*Dennis Kinslow, loan officer, Trident Mortgage Co., Rosemont, Pennsylvania*

Skill Set   Financial knowledge, communication and computer skills, sales ability, understanding of real estate transactions.

Training Needed   License required in most states. Courses and designation available through the Mortgage Bankers Association. Start with a retail bank and benefit from company training.

Earning Potential   According to an MBA survey, loan officers on full commission have a median income of $95,600. Those with a base salary have a median income of $66,200. Loan counselors have an average annual salary of $40,070, according to the Bureau of Labor Statistics.

Pluses   Similar skills as residential sales. Less involvement in solving customers' problems. More regular hours and income.

Minuses   Requires constant client cultivation. Initial difficulty in establishing credibility with former competitors. Lots of pressure to keep the deal moving.

For a state-by-state summary of real estate–related activities you can perform with your current license, check out the *ARELLO Digest of Real Estate License Laws and Current Issues* at the library of your local REALTOR® association, or order it at www.arello.org.

Sources: Inside Mortgage Finance Publications, Bethesda, Md.; Dennis Kinslow; Lender Careers (www.lendercareers.com); 2006 Mortgage Bankers Association Compensation Survey, Washington, D.C.; and Response Mortgage Services, Poulsbo, Wash.

Time to Change Companies? Ask These 10 Questions

Work's no fun when you don't like your office environment. But before you pack up and change companies, ask yourself:

1. What do you like most about your current situation?

2. What do you like least?

3. Do you receive the support services you view as most important to your success? If not, could you get them elsewhere?

4. Is your company helping you succeed? More specifically, what could the company do to help you succeed? Is your company willing to try?

5. Fill in the blanks to compare your ideal work environment with your current environment. My ideal company is _____ and my company is _____. My ideal manager is _____ and my manager is _____.

6. What event or string of events would make you change companies? Are any of those things happening in your current situation?

7. If you're considering moving to a specific company, what about it appeals to you?

8. What concerns would you have about changing companies?

9. Have you encountered a recurring problem at your company? If so, is it possible you're creating the problem and could help resolve it?

10. Are the problems at your company resolvable? If you're not sure, would you be willing to discuss them with your broker, office manager, or co-workers?

Sources: Adapted from *Recruiting and Retaining Highly Successful Agents* by NAR and Laurie Moore-Moore, The Institute for Luxury Home Marketing (www.luxury homemarketing.com), Dallas.

8 Ways to Enhance Your Web Site

To help ensure your site is a destination and not just a "click-through" for passing surfers:

1. *Target a niche.* It's nearly impossible to connect with everyone in your market, so choose a specific audience. Start by identifying something you're passionate about—like working with first-time buyers or selling waterfront properties—and craft your content around that niche.

2. *Center on your audience.* Instead of writing all about you, tell customers what's in it for them. Focus on how your services will make their lives easier. Turn every "I" on your site into a "you." If you include a bio on your site, keep it brief and use bullet points to list career highlights; bullets are easier to scan on the web.

3. *Humanize the site.* Use engaging copy and headlines and provide video tours of your market.

4. *Make compelling offers.* Put yourself in the shoes of prospective customers to create tools and offers that appeal to your niche. Offer valuable tips and resources people can use as they buy or sell.

5. *Speak their language.* Mold your writing to your target audience. It makes sense to explain basic real estate terms to first-time home buyers, but that approach may seem insulting to prospects in a high-end or second-home niche. And remember to edit MLS property descriptions to remove abbreviations the general public likely doesn't understand.

6. *Add online discussion forums.* Create a sense of community by allowing your web site visitors to post comments or questions, which you can answer online. It shows off your expertise in real estate and technology, and it keeps visitors interested. However, this tool works only if you have a well-planned niche and visitors share similar interests.

7. *Respect consumers' privacy.* Add privacy assurances on every form and survey at the site.

8. *Make navigation a breeze.* You'll ensure your site is visitor friendly by offering a site map, search engine, and automatic updates of new properties.

Sources: Michael J. Russer, a.k.a. Mr. Internet (www.russer.com), Internet consultant and speaker, Santa Barbara, Calif.; and Jon Krabbe, web strategist, Agent Image Inc. (www.agentimage.com), Marina del Ray, Calif.

5 Weeks to Better Computer Skills: Study Guide

Finally ready to jump on board with the latest computer technologies? Follow these steps and in five weeks you'll be on your way to achieving computer competence.

Week 1

Take Inventory   Ask yourself: What computer hardware and software do I use? How skilled am I on the Internet? Am I comfortable communicating via e-mail?

Once you've identified your shortcomings, seek training so that you can use your existing tech tools to their fullest. If you rely on generic software, such as Microsoft Office, find online training at the software web site. For real estate industry-specific software, such as Top Producer (www.topproducer.com), check with your local association to see if training is available and schedule the time for it.

Are you taking full advantage of your local MLS's software or tools? Contact the MLS or your local REALTOR® association to inquire about training. Often, it's free.

Week 2

Develop a Technology Plan   Determine what you want to accomplish this year. More listings? More repeat customers? Once you determine your goals, you can find software to help you reach them. You may benefit from money-management software, like Quicken (www.quicken.com), which eases accounting and financial planning, or maybe you need to invest in software that helps you track prospects.

Look at your hardware needs, too. Would a handheld device

or Tablet PC make you more efficient when you're away from the office?

Week 3

Begin the Path toward Becoming an e-PRO®   Now that you know what tools you need, gain more knowledge of your options as you start working toward your e-PRO® certification (www.epronar.com), which can be completed online in four to six weeks.

You'll learn about hardware and software options that would be a good fit for your needs and will connect with other professionals who can recommend tools or keep you from repeating their mistakes. The courses will also teach you how to use the web to reach prospects and how to use e-mail for marketing and risk reduction.

Join an online forum such as RealTalk (http://realtalk.internet crusade.com) to network with other real estate professionals and keep up to date on national trends.

Week 4

Get Your Own Domain Name   By registering for a domain name, you get a unique e-mail address that won't change if you switch your Internet service provider. Plus, it projects a more professional image than a free e-mail account.

By using an e-mail forwarding service, your e-mail address can reflect your own name (*John@JohnSmith.com*) rather than that of an outside Internet service provider (*John@hotmail.com*).

You also get an address for your web site—whether or not you have one yet. A domain that features your name or your market, such as mytownrealestate.com, is best, as it will always identify you even if your company changes.

If you don't have a web site, now is the time to begin planning for one that caters to your niche.

Use skills you learned in e-PRO® training to interview web site developers and set goals for your site.

Week 5

Incorporate Your Domain Name in Marketing   If you have a site, promote it on business cards, billboards, and other marketing materials. Fully incorporate your web site into your marketing strategy to deliver a consistent message.

Follow Up   Don't let your knowledge get stale. Make sure you really understand how your web site works, and learn how to add consumer-friendly features like virtual tours. Take advantage of training seminars, and be in the know about the latest productivity tools. Your goal should be to stay ahead of the competition.

Source: Saul Klein, president, InternetCrusade (www.internetcrusade.com), San Diego, and co-author of *Real Estate Technology Guide: Winning with Technology* (Dearborn Real Estate Education, 2004).

Checklist: 8 Essentials for a Productive Home Office

Working from home has its perks, but it also has drawbacks—namely, the tendency to get sidetracked with nonwork obligations. These are the ingredients for a professional escape where you can really get business done.

■ *A room that works*. Before you decide where your home office will be, evaluate every room in your home. For each room, ask yourself: Will distractions be kept to a minimum? Is there ample lighting? Is there enough room for all my equipment, files, and supplies? Are there enough electrical outlets? Would it be difficult to run a phone line and Internet access wiring into this space?

■ *Quality furniture.* You don't have to spend a fortune to have a presentable office. When purchasing furniture, look for an ergonomically correct desk and chair. Function matters more than appearance. If space is limited, an armoire with space for your computer equipment is ideal. Measure your space before you buy; you may see a desk or filing cabinet that fits your decor but is too large for the room.

■ *A reliable phone and messaging system.* When people call your home office and you're not there, are they getting a professional response? Consider forwarding your business line to your cell phone when you leave your office so you don't miss important calls. Use an effective voice mail system, and check your outgoing message after you record it to make sure you're the only voice and sound on the recording.

■ *A computer and printer.* Buy the best you can afford. A slow computer can cost more in lost business than it would to upgrade or replace. Add a backup system—CD-ROM, Zip, Jaz, or tape drive—to back up the irreplaceable information stored on your computer. Back up your data daily or weekly, depending on how often you use the computer. A quality printer also is a must. The most potent image some prospects will have of your company is what you send them, so whatever leaves your office needs to be top-notch.

■ *An easy-to-use filing system.* Use hanging folders for main, general categories and interior manila folders. The maximum number of documents you want in each interior file folder is about 20 sheets. Periodically go through your files and toss papers that you no longer use. Remember, the easier it is to use your filing system, the more you'll use it.

■ *An effective planner and organizer.* Whether paper-based, computerized, or electronic, you need a planning system so that you can keep track of daily and weekly tasks and store client information. A good system ensures you remember your appointments and lets you retrieve client data quickly.

■ *A place to store stationery and extra supplies.* Store such items in a closet, on shelves, or in drawers. Group supplies by type so that you have only one place to look for that type of item. Save money by buying in bulk, but buy only what you have room to store.

■ *Other tech tools you use often.* How often do you use a fax machine or copier? If the answer is not often, then don't bother making a purchase. But if you need to use them many times each day or week, do some research on different models and buy one that fits your budget and your specific needs. A multi-function machine that combines faxing, printing, scanning, and copying capabilities may be your best space-saving bet. But, remember, if it breaks down, you'll lose all its functionality for as long as it's being repaired.

Source: Lisa Kanarek, author of four books on working from home and founder of HomeOfficeLife.com, Dallas.

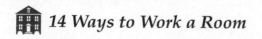 *14 Ways to Work a Room*

Whether it's a business meeting or a social event, you're always interacting with prospects. Knowing how to meet people, make a good impression, and maneuver yourself gracefully in any situation will help you succeed. These tips will let you better work any room you enter.

1. *Set your goal for any event before you arrive.* What do you want to accomplish? Maybe it's to meet five new people. Maybe it's to set three follow-up meetings. Whatever the outcome you want to achieve from the event, use your time judiciously to achieve the goal.

2. *Walk in and shake hands with confidence.* If you start with a positive attitude and a confident posture, people will be drawn to you. Offer a strong handshake with thumbs locked; don't grab fingertips or knuckles. Look the person in the eyes. Say your name slowly.

3. *Eat first.* Don't try to eat, drink, and mingle all at once.

4. *Be ready to greet.* Keep your drink in your left hand so that you're always ready to shake hands with your right hand and greet people.

5. *Start conversations.* Say hello, introduce yourself, and ask people how they're associated with the event and why they're attending. Be authentic.

6. *Get the name.* When you meet people, make sure you catch their name, and use it in conversation. It's a sign of respect. Be sure to call people by the name they've given you, for example, Mrs. Jones, Charles, or Mary Louise.

7. *Keep the conversation going.* To avoid uncomfortable pauses, use this formula: (1) Ask a question of the person you're talking to; (2) make a statement about yourself; and then (3) ask another question. Try to strike a balance between asking questions and making statements so that you avoid a third-degree interrogation or talking too much about yourself.

8. *Repeat what you've heard.* Using phrases such as "When you said a moment ago that" or "You mentioned that" proves you were paying attention.

9. *Don't let your eyes or thoughts stray.* There's nothing worse than scanning the room and not looking at the person you're talking with.

10. *Exit a conversation gracefully.* At business and social events, one of the biggest fears is getting stuck in a conversation. When you feel the interaction should end, say, "It was great talking to you. I hope you enjoy the rest of the evening."

11. *Make a request.* If your goal is to establish a relationship that will eventually turn into a deal or a referral, you need to have a reason to reconnect. Before leaving the conversation, clue people in to expect the follow-up. Say, "Can I e-mail you so that we can get together to share those great web sites?"

12. *Don't be touchy-feely.* Hugging and kissing don't belong in a business or networking situation.

13. *Leave just one card.* When you give people your business card, don't supply multiple cards for them to hand out to their friends. One card is personal and says, "This is for you."

14. *Exit the event with grace.* When leaving an event, allow 15 minutes to say good-bye to people you met. Don't just make a dash for the door.

Sources: Susan Fignar, Pur-sue Inc. (www.pur-sue.com), Itasca, Ill.; Miriam Bamberger Grogan, The Flourishing Company LLC, Silver Spring, Md.; and Rosalie Maggio, author of *The Art of Talking to Anyone* (McGraw-Hill, 2005) and *How to Say It* (Prentice Hall, 2001).

The 6 Habits Billionaires Have

Set your goals high for your real estate career by mirroring the habits of the truly elite few. According to *Forbes* magazine's annual list of "The World's Richest People," which ranks billionaires, 79 out of the world's 793 billionaires made their fortunes primarily or partially through real estate. Here's what you can learn from their habits, lifestyles, and business styles:

■ *Go commercial*. Billionaires who make their fortunes in real estate don't do it by selling one home at a time. They do it by owning and operating office buildings, shopping centers, apartment complexes, and luxury hotels.

■ *Do more than invest*. Buying a piece of property and sitting back and waiting for it to appreciate in value is not the way to make billions. You need to enhance its value. The late J. Paul Getty did just that after he bought New York's Pierre Hotel for $2.35 million in 1938 and turned it into a hub for New York society by convincing a prominent socialite to stay there. He increased the value of the investment by more than eight times.

■ *Be able to see the property for what it could be*. Just because you buy a shopping complex doesn't mean that's the best use of the property. Recognizing that real estate will have a greater value with an alternative use is what helped billionaire Laurence Tisch, now deceased, achieve success when he acquired controlling interest in the Loew's Theatres chain and converted prime Manhattan property into the Summit Hotel. Know the zoning laws in your area and apply to have properties rezoned if needed.

■ *Be tenacious and relentless*. Billionaires don't let obstacles or pitfalls keep them from achieving their goals. Just because you fail doesn't mean you can't succeed in the end. Kirk Kerkorian, whose many ventures have included ownership of Las Vegas real estate, specifically hotels, has made and lost millions in many investments, but he refuses to give up and always gets back in the game and continues to make deals.

■ *Have a thick skin.* People are by nature resentful and jealous of successful people. Don't let criticism of your work deter you from your goals.

■ *Have superior information.* If you do more research than your competitors, you'll have an advantage in any transaction.

Sources: Martin Fridson, *Leverage World*, an investment research publication, and author of *How to Be a Billionaire* (John Wiley & Sons, 2001); and *Forbes* magazine's "The World's Richest People," March 2006.

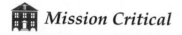 *Mission Critical*

What qualities help top performers eclipse competitors? There's no single bullet—just the steady application of these skills:

■ *Focus.* Plan your daily schedule around four moneymaking activities: prospecting, following up on leads, making presentations, and negotiating contracts.

■ *Humor.* Nothing cuts the ice better during an initial meeting or stressful negotiation.

■ *Creativity.* At least once a year, implement a new idea to attract buyers and sellers.

■ *Introspection.* Reflect on your actions and demeanor, so you'll know how others perceive you.

- *Assertiveness.* Make questions such as, "If I bring you an acceptable offer today, are you prepared to take it?" a regular part of your repertoire.

- *Standards.* Operate in an honest, professional manner and expect the same of others, including your clients and customers.

- *Attention.* Ask questions and listen to the answers—not just the words but the motivation behind them.

Sources: Howard Brinton, Star Power Systems (www.gostarpower.com), Boulder, Colo.; Danielle Kennedy, Danielle Kennedy Productions (www.daniellekennedy .com), Pacific Palisades, Calif.; and David Knox, David Knox Productions Inc. (www.davidknox.com), Minneapolis.

7 Steps to Jump-Start Your Career

New in the business? To get on the right career track from the get-go:

1. *Associate with a quality company.* Do your due diligence. Make sure the office is convenient and offers ample parking. Check whether the atmosphere is congenial, allowing you to spend time with seasoned pros. Ask about support services and training.

2. *Adjust your work timetable to your prospects' needs.* While you're proving yourself, people will expect you to respond according to their needs.

3. *Give prospects multiple ways to reach you.* Send business cards and e-mail announcements about your new career to everyone you know, set up a web site, and place ads in area publications.

4. *Master products and prices in your market.* In New York City, cooperative apartments are more prevalent than condos;

the opposite rings true in Chicago. Learn what's available, how products differ, and why one home went for $150,000 while a similar home went for almost double that price.

5. *Take the high ground.* Comments such as "but everyone does it" or "what they don't know won't hurt them" should raise your antennae. Example: If someone tells you to avoid listing past problems on a sellers' disclosure statement, don't.

6. *Keep learning.* Stay abreast of what's new, from financing options to legislative and regulatory changes. Designation programs, such as the NATIONAL ASSOCIATION OF REALTORS® Graduate, REALTOR® Institute, (REALTOR .org/GRI), are a good way to continue your education.

7. *Give back.* When you come up for air, decide how you can give back to your community.

Source: Kenneth W. Edwards, Professional Associates, Corvallis, Ore., and author of *Your Successful Real Estate Career*, 4th ed. (AMACOM, 2003).

7 *Things to Consider When Looking for a Mentor*

Whether you're being mentored or acting as a mentor, you reap rich rewards from the relationship, says Barry Spencer, director of business development with Leaders Legacy Inc., an Atlanta company specializing in training mentors. He offers the following tips for choosing a mentor.

- *Find someone you respect and trust.* Integrity and character are the most important qualities to look for.

- *Look for a person who's interested in a relationship.* A mentor needs to be open and willing to relate to you, since you'll eventually discuss both professional and personal issues.

- *Focus on a mentor who has the time and the willingness to spend with you.* A lack of time is the No. 1 reason people give for not wanting to mentor others, says Spencer. You can help by being flexible and fitting into your mentor's schedule.

- *Look beyond your door.* Although a top real estate practitioner may be a great mentor, you can also learn about business principles, and perhaps get a new perspective, from a professional outside of real estate.

- *Don't expect the mentor to be a magician.* Mentors can give you new insights, but they won't solve all your personal or business problems. A good mentor will direct you to other sources of assistance for special problems.

- *Opt for openness.* Good mentors let you into their world, sharing both professional and personal triumphs and failures.

- *Don't expect instant results.* Mentoring is a journey. As long as you're learning something you didn't know before, the mentoring relationship is working. Persevere. "Mentoring takes as long as it takes," says Spencer.

🏠 9 Key Rookie Mistakes

Real estate is harder than it looks, as many rookies learn. But even experienced sales associates can fall into bad habits. Here are some traps to avoid, and ways to spring yourself if you've slipped.

1. *Neglecting to develop a business plan and then to work the plan.* A salesperson without concrete goals and timelines is

likely to flounder. Without a plan, salespeople too often allocate funds and time in ways that don't pay off, says Ruth Marcus, training director with Russell & Jeffcoat, REALTORS®, in Columbia, South Carolina.

2. *Failing to create a consistent marketing look and not sticking to it.* New associates often waste money on advertising and promotion without focusing on what will really generate business, says Marcus.

3. *Forgetting to purchase equipment, such as computers, as a business entity.* Buying equipment as a business instead of as an individual allows you to depreciate equipment over a five- or seven-year period and deduct that depreciation from your income taxes. Also, as a business, you can generally access business customer service when you have a technology problem. Often this is much more responsive than tech help lines for consumers, says Terry Watson, president of Watson World Corporation in Chicago.

4. *Putting off prospecting or lead generating.* Generating leads should be an everyday task for sales associates. When she's working with new recruits, Jan Brand, director of career development at Ebby Halliday, REALTORS®, in Dallas, tells new sales associates that they need to make 30 contacts a day, five days a week. Lead generation can include phone calls, handwritten notes, and mailing to one's sphere of influence, as well as networking.

5. *Ignoring the training and other resources your brokerage has to offer.* Sales associates need to keep up-to-date on industry changes and continually work to improve their business and selling skills, regardless of their tenure in the business, says Brand.

6. *Failing to work their sphere of influence.* It's much harder to get business from a new customer than from a repeat one, says Marcus, so it's critical to stay in touch with past customers, friends, and contacts.

7. *Having no accountability.* Being held accountable helps people stay focused. If you don't feel as if you're getting the feedback you need, take the initiative and set up regular meetings with your mentor or broker. Also make yourself accountable to customers by providing written guidelines on exactly what services you'll provide for them, suggests Frank Cook in his book *21 Things I Wish My Broker Had Told Me* (Dearborn Real Estate Education, 2002).

8. *Being paralyzed by what you don't know.* Marcus says that she sees some new salespeople who worry so much about not understanding every aspect of a contract or a disclosure form that they postpone prospecting. Although education is crucial for sales associates at all levels, rookies should remember that they can rely on their brokers, sales managers, or company attorney for answers, says Marcus.

9. *Failing to have enough resources to establish yourself.* It isn't only living expenses, says Marcus. New sales associates also need funds for marketing themselves and any listings they get. She recommends having six months' income in reserve, more if you don't have a spouse that works. After each closing, set aside funds to reinvest in your business. And don't forget to put money aside for income taxes, cautions Brand.

More: Mark Leader's *Red Hot Rookie,* available at the Real Estate Bookshelf at REALTOR.org.

🏠 *6 Steps to Successful Public Speaking*

Public speaking is the cheapest form of advertising around. So choose a topic you know a lot about and find an audience. Here's how to win an ovation:

1. *Don't try to cover it all.* People absorb less when they listen than when they read, so don't overwhelm them. Organize your speech around three main topic points. For each point, have your facts straight before you enter the room.

2. *Get them laughing.* Starting with an anecdote or joke will warm up the audience. Find some great real estate–related humor in the Facilitator Resources in the "Prepackaged Sales Meetings" at REALTOR® Magazine Online (REALTOR.org/realtormag).

3. *Use visual aids.* If you're comfortable working with Power-Point, create a presentation, then offer to send copies to anyone who gives you a name and address. Or highlight the main points on a handout, so participants don't have to take notes.

4. *Vary the speed and pitch of your voice* to avoid monotony and to make your presentation seem more dynamic.

5. *Visualize yourself giving a great speech,* your voice clear and assured, your audience rapt. It will help calm your nerves and give you confidence.

6. *Practice, practice, practice.* Run through your speech and any visual aids several times, so that you feel comfortable. If

possible, get to the room ahead of time to learn the setup and practice with the microphone.

Sources: Roxanne Lee, Nancy B. Edmiston & Associates LLC, Pearce, Ariz. (in "Stand and Deliver," by Marcia Layton Turner, REALTOR® Magazine, May 2003); Walter Sanford, "When You're On Stage . . . You're Selling," REALTOR® Magazine Online, 2002; and Toastmasters International (www.toastmasters.org).

Where to Speak

- Senior citizen centers.
- Condominium boards.
- Health clubs.
- Garden clubs.
- School assemblies and clubs.
- Book clubs.
- Investment clubs.
- Professional and cultural groups.

To solicit speaking engagements, send a brief resume, a list of other speaking engagements, and two or three suggested topics to the program chair or president of each organization. Space speaking engagements out so that people don't get tired of hearing from you.

Compiled by REALTOR® Magazine's editorial staff.

What to Talk About: Pick a Topic That Fits Your Audience

- Home buying for first-time buyers.
- Preparing your home for sale.
- Owning versus renting.
- Selecting a second home.
- Selecting a site for retirement.
- Preparing your home to accommodate aging in place.
- Renovations that pay off. Use the "Cost vs. Value Report" for tips. (The Report is produced by *Remodeling* magazine, www.remodeling.hw.net).
- The fastest-growing neighborhoods in your area.
- New zoning or real estate–related regulations in your area.
- Becoming a landlord; income from rental properties.

TIP Very few people are natural public speakers. Consider investing in a few sessions with a speech or drama coach from your local community college to improve your presentation.

TIP If you're not sure about public speaking, try it out by being part of a panel discussion. It's less pressure since you're not going solo.

Compiled by REALTOR® Magazine's editorial staff.

5 Tips for Great Public Speaking

Whether it's a listing presentation, public hearing, or business meeting:

- *Garner credibility in the first minute*. Make eye contact, speak slowly, and articulate how you'll address the needs and concerns of the audience.

- *Stay in real time.* Focus on what you're trying to say instead of thinking ahead to what you want to say next.

- *Repeat important points.* Effective communication is about what listeners remember.

- *Use positive language.* If you say, "This is not a problem situation; I wouldn't worry that this will turn into a disaster," what the listener hears is "problem," "worry," and "disaster." If you mean "Everything will be just fine," then say it.

- *Factual information should be written down.* Use verbal communication to motivate and persuade. Statistics and other factual information are more easily digested in printed material.

Sources: Thom Brockett, Long & Foster Real Estate Inc., Bethesda, Md.; Don Patrick, CreatePlus Inc., Seattle; and Kay Peters, KTT Communications, New York.

Building a 7th-Level Business

When you start in real estate sales, generating your own business and handling your own administration, you're at what can be called a first-level business. Reach for a seventh-level business by progressively adding assistants and then other staff to free you up for higher-level activity.

LEVEL	SALES AND MARKETING	ADMINISTRATION AND PROCESSING
First	You	You
Second	You	First assistant
Third	You	Marketing/bookkeeping staff, transaction coordinator

Fourth	You, lead buyer agent	Marketing/bookkeeping staff, transaction coordinator
Fifth	You, lead buyer agent, buyer agents, listing specialist	Marketing/bookkeeping staff, telemarketer, listing manager, transaction coordinator
Sixth (You: CEO)	Buyer agents, lead buyer agent, listing specialists, lead listing specialist	Marketing/bookkeeping staff, telemarketer, listing manager, transaction coordinator
Seventh (You: owner)	Buyer agents, lead buyer agent, listing specialists, lead listing specialist	CEO, marketing/bookkeeping staff, telemarketer, listing manager, transaction coordinator, lead coordinator

Adapted from *The Millionaire Real Estate Agent* (McGraw-Hill, 2004) by Gary Keller with Dave Jenks and Jay Papasan; copyright © 2004 by Rellek Publishing Partners.

10 Facts about the NAR Code of Ethics

1. Establishing ethical standards for real estate practitioners was the reason for organizing the national association.

2. The Code of Ethics—adopted in 1913—was one of the first codifications of ethical duties adopted by any business group and was modeled on ethical codes of physicians, engineers, and lawyers.

3. The Code was the precursor of state license laws.

4. The Code embodies the Golden Rule: "Whatsoever ye would do that others should do to you, do you even so to them."

5. The Code ensures that consumers are served by requiring REALTORS® to cooperate with each other in furthering clients' best interests.

6. The Code demands respect for others' exclusive relationships with clients.

7. The Code keeps disputes between members "in the family" by requiring REALTORS® to arbitrate.

8. The Code is enforced at the local level through knowledgeable peer panels.

9. The Code consists of 17 Articles, and approximately 75 supporting Standards of Practice and 133 explanatory case interpretations. The numbers change as updates are made.

10. The Code is a living document subject to ongoing review to ensure it stays relevant. An updated version appears every January in REALTOR® Magazine. It's also available at REALTOR.org.

Source: NAR's Professional Standards Committee.

5 Practical Money-Saving Ideas

1. *Put aside a set amount per week (say $20) from your wallet.* Or just save your pocket change in a jar.

2. *Focus on recurring expenses.* It's fine to clip grocery coupons, but your return will be greater if you do things like shop around your monthly auto insurance, suggests Kaja Whitehouse in *The Wall Street Journal*.

3. *Round up the amounts you spend when you balance your checkbook.* Gradually you'll build up a surplus you can transfer to savings, suggests Liz Pulliam Weston with MSN Money.

4. *Buy a nice, new used car.* Yes, you need a good ride for selling real estate, but you can save an average of $1,799 a year

over five years by buying a used car, estimates online car site www.edmunds.com. To be sure you don't have a lemon, check out www.carfax.com, which provides a vehicle history for a fee.

5. *Pay bills on time.* To avoid hefty late fees, set up due dates for bills in your contact manager tickler file, then pay on time.

Compiled by REALTOR® Magazine's editorial staff.

🏛 *Tax Records You Can't Do Without*

Keep most of these tax records for a minimum of three years* (the time the IRS has to audit you):

- Your filed tax returns and supporting documentation, such as receipts and records of initial stock costs.

- Deposit slips that show gross income, as well as Form 1099s you receive from your broker.

- Vendor bills for equipment you use for business, along with canceled checks or credit card slips to show payment.

- Copies of medical and dental bills, especially if they amount to more than 7.5 percent of your income and qualify for a medical deduction.

- Copies of your quarterly tax payment forms, along with the canceled checks.

- Trip sheets for business use of your car.

Note: If there's fraud, the IRS will ask for six years' worth of records. Keep returns permanently.

- Depreciation worksheets showing deductions you take on business equipment.

- Cost of improvements you make to your home or business office (can't be deducted, but can be added to the property's basis).

- Support for business entertainment deductions, including the business purpose of the expense, the business relationship of the person entertained, and the time and place of the expenditure.

- Documents that show your tax basis for property you inherited or received as a gift.

Sources: TurboTax (www.turbotax.com); *The Wall Street Journal*; and Internal Revenue Service (www.irs.gov).

5 Best Real Estate Stats to Track

Wondering how to become your market's top information expert? Keep tabs on the following data:

1. *Household composition and age trends.* Family size plays a big factor in the types of homes that are in demand. A significant increase in a particular age category may give you an idea of a market segment to target or a segment of the population that's entering a different phase of the buying cycle. Visit the U.S. Census Bureau (www.census.gov) for demographic information.

2. *Changes in zoning or additions to local infrastructure.* These may be indicators of a change in use in an area or the availability of yet-undeveloped land. Either could have a significant effect on property values or new inventory on the market.

3. *Affordability indices.* Affordability, which the NATIONAL ASSOCIATION OF REALTORS® tracks monthly by region, looks at area incomes in relation to area median home prices, which will help you predict the universe of buyers out there. Search by "Housing Affordability Index" at REALTOR.org.

4. *Employment trends by industry sector.* Beyond general unemployment numbers, performance by industry, tracked by the Bureau of Labor Statistics (www.bls.gov), is useful if your area depends on certain industries for jobs.

5. *Remodeling spending.* This data, tracked by Harvard University's Joint Center for Housing Studies (www.jchs.harvard.edu), may indicate whether people are moving up or staying in place.

Also check with state and local economic development agencies and universities for more localized data.

Compiled by REALTOR® Magazine's editorial staff.

Chapter 7

TIME MANAGEMENT

Don't Sweat the Unimportant Stuff

The Rolling Stones were wrong. Time is not on your side. It's finite and fleeting. But there are simple ways to make better use of your time, says Stephen R. Covey, vice chairman and co-founder of FranklinCovey Company, a business training and consulting business in Salt Lake City. "All you have to do is say yes to what's important and no to what's urgent and not important," he says. "It's the urgent but not important stuff that consumes half of people's lives."

Stever Robbins of The Stever Robbins Company, a Cambridge, Massachusetts, firm that specializes in executive development, agrees. "I worked with a manager of a billion-dollar company, who manages to get through his e-mail every day," Robbins says. "But he goes through it in order. Instead, I had him scan his inbox, flag the messages that were most important, and answer those first. He realized that everything was important, but three e-mails would give him 10 times the payback than the others, so he needed to make sure those got taken care of first."

Like prioritizing e-mail, you'll get more bang for your time by concentrating on your highest-leverage activities, Robbins says.

"Many people spend a lot of time on activities that don't move the business forward, such as doing administrative work," he says. Let others handle those tasks. Instead, if you get your best leads from personal referrals, spend time establishing strong relationships.

Covey says real estate practitioners "are focused on short-term results and numbers and making this deal or that deal, and they don't build a reputation so that their clients become their sales force. Instead of taking the expedient route, take the long-term approach for service and integrity."

Here's more on how to manage your time to ensure long-term success.

10 Ways to Stop Wasting Time

Distractions can extend the amount of time you spend at work. Use these tips to increase your efficiency, become more productive, and get more from life.

1. *Set goals.* Write down specific objectives for the year—"I will sell X number of houses per month in order to sell Y houses this year"—and review them regularly.

2. *Make a plan.* Break your goals down into more manageable tasks and assign deadlines to each task.

3. *Push through barriers.* When your productivity is lagging, be solution-oriented. If you lack resources, talk with your broker or engage help from team members. If political issues stand in your way, insist on open communications. If work priorities are unclear, talk with your manager or team members.

4. *Create a weekly plan.* At the start of each week, review your goals and determine three or four actions that would sig-

nificantly impact your business. Then plan meetings, appointments, and tasks accordingly. Prioritize associated tasks in order of importance.

5. *Organize every day.* Take 10 minutes every morning to focus on the most important goals, tasks, and appointments for the day. Write them down and prioritize them.

6. *Simplify your work.* Every month, put into practice one new step or system to simplify the way you do your work. Having systems for updating your database, sending prospect letters, handling tenant requests, and so on will save you time and alleviate stress and frustration.

7. *Use an integrated, mobile planning system.* Whether you use a paper planner, handheld device, or both, make sure your information sources are synched and with you at all times.

8. *Review your progress.* On a weekly basis, look back at how well you worked your plan. Figure out what's not working and fix it.

9. *Learn to say no courteously.* When others come to you with problems that prevent you from finishing vital tasks, politely turn them away by arranging a meeting in the future or referring them to someone else who can help. Engage a manager who helps you identify which priorities you should tackle first.

10. *Delegate and partner.* Don't try to do it all yourself. Hire a virtual assistant, ask your broker whether the staff receptionist can help with your mailing, or team up with another professional to share weekend responsibilities.

Source: FranklinCovey (www.franklincovey.com), Salt Lake City.

6 Distractions, and How to Avoid Them

Here are solutions to common time traps.

1. *Negative office mates.* In just about every office, there's a salesperson who's unhappy about something. It's easy to be drawn into conversations that amount to little more than complaining, especially when the discussion doesn't involve the person who can affect change. *Solution:* Set a personal policy that you won't discuss issues with anyone other than those who are directly involved or can make a change.

2. *Indecisive buyers.* Buyers can take up a lot of your time, particularly if they're constantly calling with questions or additional properties to visit. *Solution:* Create a plan and schedule time for prospecting and appointments. Then stick to the plan. If buyers are taking a long time making a decision, offer to e-mail them a weekly schedule of open houses and new listings that meet their criteria, and ask them to call you when they're ready to get serious about buying.

3. *The inability to say no.* Everyone wants to be liked by colleagues, but some salespeople, particularly rookies eager to please, might find they're spending too much time on things that aren't productive to their own business. *Solution:* Look at the plan for your business and determine whether an activity will help you reach your goals. If not, then just say no.

4. *Too many tasks.* Often, when people are faced with too many things that need their attention, they become overwhelmed and don't do anything. *Solution:* Create a to-do list for the following day. As items are accomplished, highlight them rather than cross them out, so you'll focus on what you fin-

ished rather than what you didn't. Have confidence that you can handle everything you need to do.

5. *Demanding sellers.* Sellers can be a time drain, constantly calling with questions and other interruptions, particularly if they feel you're not doing your job. *Solution:* Create a communication schedule to provide regular updates and status reports. Be proactive, not reactive. If sellers are calling you more than you're calling them, it's a red flag that you're not servicing their needs the way they expect.

6. *Unrealistic promises.* When you fail to carry through on a promised action, it creates a ripple effect that can spread quickly through your business, requiring time to clean up the mess that could have been spent in more productive ways. *Solution:* Make sure you follow through on everything you promise. Say what you mean and mean what you say.

Source: Darryl Davis, Darryl Davis Seminars Inc. (www.darryldavisseminars.com), Wading River, N.Y.

15 Ways to Manage Your Time More Efficiently

1. Spend the first 15 minutes of every day, or the last 15 minutes at night, making a to-do list.
2. Decide what times of day you're the most productive, and schedule your most difficult jobs then.
3. Use waiting time effectively by planning small tasks you can do in short segments of time.
4. Build flexibility into your schedule so you can adapt when things don't go according to schedule or new opportunities arise.

5. When you return a phone call, minimize phone tag by including a time you can be reached.

6. Spend the most time on the job that produces the most income.

7. Don't let nonproductive tasks consume your time.

8. Take a break to refresh yourself; you'll be more productive.

9. Split longer tasks into smaller increments to allow you to fit them into available time.

10. Divide a difficult job into several parts so that you don't burn out before it's done, suggests Max Messmer in *Business Credit* magazine (June 2000).

11. Set completion dates for tasks to avoid procrastination.

12. Create a system to prioritize tasks, but plan on reevaluating priorities daily.

13. Reward yourself with 15 minutes of fun after completing a difficult job.

14. Delegate routine chores, but be sure you train your helpers well.

15. Value your time, and ask others to do the same.

Source: REALTOR® Magazine Online's (REALTOR.org/realtormag) "Better Time Management" Sales Meeting.

🏠 *11 Steps to a Clutter-Free Zone*

A messy work environment is not conducive to peak productivity. Here are some ways to get rid of the piles taking up valuable desk space.

1. *Reduce your reading pile.* Rather than keep entire publications, tear out the articles you want to read and discard the

rest. Take reading material with you whenever you leave the office.

2. *Pare down large piles first.* Concentrate particularly on large, bulky items. You'll see immediate results and be motivated to keep going.

3. *Sort piles into categories.* Assign items to action-oriented categories, such as to do, to read, or to file, and then actually perform the assigned task.

4. *Open your mail over a shredder or recycling bin.* Make an immediate decision on how best to deal with each item, and you're more likely to avoid creating piles in the first place.

5. *Create a "consider" file.* Put items that require more time and consideration into a file so they don't clutter your work space. Make an appointment each week to review the contents of the file.

6. *Set a disposal date.* If you haven't read something within a reasonable amount of time, say, two months, you probably aren't going to read it. If you find yourself regularly discarding the same publication, cancel the subscription.

7. *Avoid scraps of paper.* Use a spiral notebook to keep phone messages and notes in one place.

8. *Keep organizational systems simple.* When deciding where to store items, ask yourself, "Where's the first place I'd look for this?"

9. *Organize items based on frequency of use.* Only things you use every day should be on your desk. Items you use once a week should go in your desk. Things used less frequently should be kept elsewhere, such as a storage closet.

10. *Make time to organize.* Set aside 10 minutes at the beginning or end of each day to clean up your workspace and put things in their appropriate places.

11. *Be consistent.* Staying organized is a lot easier than getting organized.

Source: Barb Myers, The Time Manager (www.ineedmoretime.com), Newark, Ohio.

10 Jobs an Assistant Can Handle

Are you bogged down in tasks that don't seem to help you achieve your goals? Then you need to leverage the talents of others to help you get the job done more efficiently, effectively, and profitably. Here are some responsibilities you can delegate to an assistant:

A licensed assistant can:

1. *Coordinate home inspections and appraisals.* That includes setting and confirming appointments, preparing paper-work, and even attending meetings with appraisers when necessary.

2. *Help with open houses and showing properties.* An assistant can schedule appointments, develop a driving route for showing properties, and even show properties when needed.

3. *Provide listing assistance.* Use an assistant to update the MLS and other databases and prepare listing packets and packets for out-of-town buyers.

4. *Facilitate closings.* That includes providing documentation for the broker and coordinating details, such as date, location, and documents needed.

5. *Write advertising copy.* Composing catchy, accurate, and legal real estate ads takes someone who fully understands the real estate business.

An unlicensed assistant can:

6. *Handle general administration.* With an assistant ordering office supplies, filing, organizing files, typing, and tidying the office, you'll be freed up to work with clients.

7. *Take on marketing tasks.* Expand your business by using a marketing assistant to develop and implement direct-mail and e-mail campaigns. Your assistant can also maintain your mailing lists, print labels, and coordinate the labeling, sorting, and bundling of mailing pieces.

8. *Route incoming phone calls.* Make sure a friendly voice answers your phone. You'll send a message that, even when you're not in the office, all your bases are covered.

9. *Maintain your database.* Developing a user-friendly and effective database is time consuming—but there's no more effective prospecting tool.

10. *Manage bills and billings.* As important as this task is, it can easily be handed off to an assistant.

Source: Howard Brinton, STAR POWER Systems (www.gostarpower.com), Boulder, Colo.

Countdown to a Carefree Vacation

Vacations help recharge your batteries and allow you to spend important time with family and friends. But if you get away only to find yourself checking your e-mail and voice mail frequently, worrying that work will dry up in your absence, and feeling you're shortchanging customers and colleagues, you haven't prepared sufficiently. Let this timeline guide you; adjust it as needed. Bon voyage!

At Least Five Weeks Out

Begin keeping assistants, colleagues, and your broker in the loop about your deals and inform your customers when you'll be away.

If you have a shared office calendar, be sure to add your vacation dates early—at the beginning of the year, if possible. The dates may change, but the heads-up helps colleagues prepare mentally.

Four Weeks Before

If you haven't already, arrange with an assistant, partner, or colleague to cover your listings, closings, and phone duty. If you like certain procedures followed, spell them out. For example: "Call current listers once a week with a status report."

If you've already lined up a backup, check with the person again to make sure his or her schedule hasn't changed so that you both won't be away at the same time. To avoid misunderstandings, decide on a mutually agreed fee for each transaction closed in your absence.

Remind other colleagues by e-mail that you plan to be gone, provide exact dates, and let them know who's covering for you and whether there are any circumstances under which they should contact you during your vacation.

Three Weeks Ahead

Remind clients and potential buyers and sellers that you're going away and give them the name and cell phone number of those covering for you. Tell clients how to contact you in case of an emergency. If you'll be out of the loop—in a jungle without cell service or an Internet café, say—take extra time to reassure them you're well covered.

Two Weeks Ahead

Give your broker and colleagues who are covering for you notes on your current listings and closings, sufficient brochures and disclosure forms, and the phone numbers of others involved in your transactions, such as co-op salespeople, loan officers, and attorneys. You may want to slip copies of this information into any open files, too.

Give your contact information to your broker and backup. You may want to provide a specific hotel name and phone number or just say, "I'll be in Santa Fe, New Mexico," and provide your cell phone number for emergencies.

One Week Ahead

Ask buyers and sellers if they have last-minute concerns that you and your colleagues should know about. Set dates to meet with prospects and clients on your return. And schedule a post-vacation meeting—perhaps over lunch or a latte—for a brain dump from co-workers who handled your work. Before you head out of town, organize future work, such as scheduling open houses, stagings, and photo shoots.

By this point, you'll know whether you really need co-workers to keep you in the loop about transactions while you're away. Broker John Mayfield is more relaxed on vacation if his assistant types up notes of the most critical goings-on and e-mails them to him daily. He also asks her to forward less important e-mail that he should read before he returns. He checks in by phone midway through his trip.

A Few Days Before

Tie up loose ends. Record a voice vacation message on your office and cell phones. Set up an out-of-office e-mail, saying, "I won't be retrieving messages while I'm away [if that's the case]. Please call my office instead. So-and-so will be happy to help during my absence." And include the person's direct number.

If you plan to stay in touch, be sure you pack your cell phone, laptop, handheld device, adapters, cords, and extra batteries.

While Away

Relax and have a great trip. Don't worry: You'll be found if a true emergency occurs. So focus on being rested for your return.

Sources: Elizabeth Ballis, Coldwell Banker Residential Brokerage, Chicago; Bob Herd, Coldwell Banker Residential Brokerage, Oro Valley, Ariz.; and John Mayfield Jr., Mayfield Real Estate Inc., Farmington, Mo.

10 Numbers to Program into Your Cell Phone

Speed dial is often the best friend of busy real estate pros. Don't waste time looking for those critical numbers when you can get help with only three digits.

1. 911 and your local number for nonemergency police calls when you need the cavalry.

2. Your office when the buyers have looked at every house you can think of and you just hope there are some new listings.

3. Your tech helper when a machine gets the better of you.

4. Your babysitter, dog walker, or other care provider when that buyer just has to take one more look.

5. Your two most trusted loan officers when you have a buyer who needs to get prequalified fast or lose the deal.

6. Your lawyer or the association legal hotline when you're not sure how to stay on the right side of the law.

7. Your local service station or car dealership when you turn the key and hear "chug."

8. Your transaction coordinator or your title company when you have only two days left until closing and you still don't have all the paperwork in.

9. Your doctor or the local hospital emergency room when the buyer trips on the stairs you told the seller six times to fix.

10. Your favorite restaurant—the one with the soothing music and the extra-large martinis—for when it's really been one of those days.

Compiled by REALTOR® Magazine's editorial staff.

19 Text Message Abbreviations You Should Know

Texting on the go? You'll want to have a few standard abbreviations in your text-message vocabulary. Just remember: Most business communication should be the more formal variety.

Text messager #1: To avoid a WOMBAT, we should ADD, AYEC, the remaining WRK. But IANAL, so PXT to the client. I know TTTT, but let's set a deadline JIC. GL & KIT.

Text messager #2: SLAP! MTF by COB. It's AAP! THNQ! TSTB on the update.

#1: UW & HAND. EOM.

Translation:

Text messager #1: To avoid a waste of money, brains, and time, we should address, at your earliest convenience, the remaining work. But I am not a lawyer, so please explain that to the client. I know these things take time, but let's set a deadline just in case. Good luck and keep in touch.

Text messager #2: Sounds like a plan! More to follow by close of business. It's always a pleasure! Thank you! The sooner the better on the update.

#1: You're welcome and have a nice day. End of message.

Compiled by REALTOR® Magazine's editorial staff.

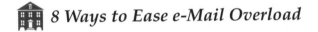 *8 Ways to Ease e-Mail Overload*

You can't control your incoming e-mail, but you can be smart about what to do with messages once they arrive. Stever Robbins of The Stever Robbins Company in Cambridge, Massachusetts, suggests these ways to ease the flow.

- *Unless the sender is a client or prospect, don't feel obligated to respond.* If you reply, you're encouraging the sender to keep sending you e-mail.

- *Be ruthless.* Fine yourself $5 every time you spend more than five seconds deciding how to handle each message. This will force you to prioritize your mail.

- *Make it harder for people to reach you.* Give out your e-mail address only to those who truly need it.

- *Create separate e-mail accounts.* Using different accounts for personal and work messages will help keep incoming mail to each address to a minimum.

- *Check e-mail only twice each day.* Explain in your signature that you don't constantly monitor your e-mail and that if people have truly important information they should call you. Or have an assistant monitor your inbox.

- *Opt out or delete.* When marketers send e-mail, by law they're required to give you an opt-out feature. Use it. If you're not sure the source is reputable, however, just delete the message.

- *Use your e-mail program's spam filters.* Keep junk e-mail from reaching you in the first place.

- *Follow the rule of three.* Once a third e-mail has been written on the same subject, that is, original message, response, second response, pick up the phone and call the other person.

🏠 *10 Must-Haves for Your Car*

Your schedule is too jammed to allow for unexpected trips to the office to retrieve key tools. Be prepared for any circumstance by always carrying these handy items.

1. Cell phone.
2. Tape measure.
3. Tape recorder to note FSBO addresses and thoughts while driving.
4. Signs to post right after nabbing a listing.
5. Spare tire (filled of course, and an aerosol can for inflating a flat tire, such as Fix-a-Flat).
6. PDA (with current MLS information).
7. Book of maps.

8. Phone books.

9. Laptop, portable printer, and power converter.

10. For clients: handy wipes, extra umbrellas, tissues, and, for kids, paper and colored pencils.

Sources: Pam Beard, BrokerSouth GMAC Real Estate, Vicksburg, Miss.; and University of Tennessee Police, www.utpolice.org.

Get Going: 8 Easy Steps

Think you may procrastinate? If you keep putting off a task, which becomes a problem when left undone, you fit the definition.

If you avoid paying bills and incur needless interest charges or put off cleaning your desk and its messiness hurts your sales production, you're procrastinating. You're not alone. Procrastinators represent a huge population. How big isn't known because most people say "I don't have time" rather than "I'm procrastinating," says Rita Emmett, author of *The Procrastinator's Handbook* (Walker & Co., 2000) and a recovering procrastinator. So read this list now, not later, to learn to get in gear.

1. *Understand that procrastination isn't a personality trait or flaw that you're born with.* It's a habit, and it's changeable.

2. *Admit to yourself that you may procrastinate.* Think about your inactions and how you rationalize why you don't do certain things. Many excuses relate to fear: doing something imperfectly, tackling the unknown, being rejected, failing, or even succeeding. Are you afraid to become a member of your Million-Dollar Club and have that as your new benchmark?

3. *Know that another reason you procrastinate may be anxiety about starting.* You may worry about how long it will take to

complete a task, fret that you don't have enough information, hate doing whatever needs to be done, or secretly like procrastinating since you equate it with gaining some power. To make getting started more tolerable, set a timer and devote one uninterrupted hour a day to tackling a particular project. Avoid distractions such as checking e-mail.

4. *Be aware of your more stressful times.* Avoid overloading yourself at these junctures. If your business tends to get very busy in spring, March may be a bad time to plan gatherings with family and friends that you've been putting off.

5. *Once you understand why—and when—you procrastinate, try to change.* If clutter derails your work, start to get organized. Get over the idea that you can't throw anything away. Pitch what you don't need in your office, on your desk, and in your car. You'll look more professional to your customers, too.

6. *Don't start a second task until you finish your first.* Avoid becoming sidetracked.

7. *Reward yourself.* Use small rewards for small jobs, bigger rewards for bigger jobs.

8. *Remember that practice makes perfect.* If you slip back into old patterns, start anew. Select one procrastinated task, set the timer, focus, do the job, and reward yourself.

If you've read to this point, congratulations: You finished the list without procrastinating.

Additional Resources

CHAPTER 1 *Prospecting*

Articles

"8 Great Giveaway Ideas" (REALTOR® Magazine Online).
> To find: Search by title at REALTOR.org/realtormag.
> (Requires NAR member login.)

"Back to Basics: REALTORS® with Staying Power" (NVAR.com *e-News Update*, March 9, 2006).
> To find: Search by title at www.nvar.com.
> Strategies, including mentoring, community outreach, and marketing, for working in changing markets.

"Best of RealTalk #4: Handling Multiple Offers" (RealTown's InternetCrusade).
> www.internetcrusade.com/articles/realtalk4.asp.

"The Good and the Bad of Multiple Offers" (*Realty Times*, Sept. 10, 2004).
> To find: Search by title at www.realtytimes.com.

"Insights into Multiple Offers" (REALTOR® Magazine Online).
> To find: Search by title at REALTOR.org/realtormag.
> (Requires NAR member login.)

"Multiple Offers in Hot Markets" (*Realty Times*, Sept. 27, 2001).
> To find: Search by title at www.realtytimes.com.

"Multiple Offers: Too Much of a Good Thing?" (REALTOR®
Magazine Online, Sept. 2004).
> To find: Search by Too Much of a Good Thing? at REALTOR
> .org/realtormag. (In results, click Law: Multiple Offers.)

"Blog and Be Seen" (*California Real Estate*, Oct. 2005).
> To find: Search by title at www.car.org.

"Blog World" (REALTOR® Magazine Online, May 2006).
> To find: Search by title at REALTOR.org/realtormag.

"Community Involvement" (REALTOR® Magazine Online).
> To find: Search by title at REALTOR.org/realtormag.
> (Requires NAR member login. You may have to scroll down to
> find link.)

"Can You Be Trusted?" (*Realty Times*, Oct. 24, 2005).
> To find: Search by title without question mark at
> www.realtytimes.com.
> If you don't build trust, consumers won't be honest with you
> about their needs.

"Get More Sales by Building Trust" (*Realty Times*, Sept. 17, 2004).
> To find: Search by title at www.realtytimes.com.

"Honesty is the Best Policy" (REALTOR® Magazine Online,
Aug. 2003).
> To find: Search by title at REALTOR.org/realtormag.

"Do You Undersell Your Own Virtual Tours?" (*Realty Times*,
June 10, 2005).
> To find: Search by title without question mark at
> www.realtytimes.com.
> Offers 10 tips for effectively cross-marketing virtual tours.

"Virtual Tour Options that Add Pizzazz" (REALTOR® Magazine
Online, May 2006).
> To find: Search by title at REALTOR.org/realtormag.

"How to Ask for Referrals" (REALTOR® Magazine Online, March 2005).

>To find: Search by title at REALTOR.org/realtormag.

"How to Capture More FSBOs by Knowing Their Style" (*Realty Times*, May 1, 2006).

>To find: Search by title at www.realtytimes.com.

"Kickstart Your Profits with Farming" (*Realty Times*, Nov. 19, 2001).

>To find: Search by title at www.realtytimes.com.

"Managers: Keeping Clients Loyal" (NVAR.com *e-News Update*, Aug. 11, 2000).

>To find: Search by Keep Your Clients Loyal at www.nvar.com.

>Use databases, mailings, the Internet, and communication to keep existing clients.

"Powerful Prelisting: 4 Prelisting Mistakes to Avoid" (REALTOR® Magazine Online).

>To find: Search by title at REALTOR.org/realtormag. (Requires username and password.)

"Prospecting a Neighborhood in a Hot Market" (*Realty Times*, Feb. 11, 2005).

>To find: Search by title at www.realtytimes.com.

"Prospecting in Print" (REALTOR® Magazine Online).

>To find: Search by title at REALTOR.org/realtormag. (Requires NAR member login.)

"Sending Audio, Video Reports to Your Real Estate Prospects" (*Realty Times*, Aug. 29, 2005).

>To find: Search by Sending Audio at www.realtytimes.com.

"Stamped for Success" (REALTOR® Magazine Online, July 2004).

>To find: Search by title at REALTOR.org/realtormag.

The U.S. Postal Service web site can help real estate professionals launch direct-mail campaigns.

"Turn Prospects into Clients" (Texas REALTOR® Online, Dec. 2000). To find: Click "News & Pubs" at www.texasrealtors.com, then *Texas REALTOR®*, and Article Archives. Then choose "December" from 2000 pull-down menu.

"Video Can Be a Powerful Lure for Customers" (REALTOR® Magazine Online, Aug. 2004). To find: Search by title at REALTOR.org/realtormag.

NATIONAL ASSOCIATION OF REALTORS® Field Guides and REALTOR® Magazine Online Sections

Field Guide to Direct Mail
REALTOR.org/libweb.nsf/pages/fg205

Field Guide to Farming and Prospecting
REALTOR.org/libweb.nsf/pages/fg204

Field Guide to Working with FSBOs
REALTOR.org/libweb.nsf/pages/fg210

Personal Marketing section
To find: Click Personal Marketing under Selling at REALTOR.org/realtormag. (Requires NAR member login.)

Prospecting section
To find: Click Prospecting under Selling at REALTOR.org/realtormag. (Requires NAR member login.)

REALTOR.org Resource

"A Buyers' and Sellers' Guide to Multiple Offer Negotiations." To find: Search by title at REALTOR.org. (Requires NAR member login.)

NATIONAL ASSOCIATION OF REALTORS®
Virtual Library eBooks Collection

Check out books online for free at ebooks.REALTOR.org. (eBooks are available to NAR members only. Access requires NAR member number.)

Advanced Selling Strategies: The Proven System of Sales Ideas, Methods, and Techniques Used by Top Salespeople Everywhere by Brian Tracy (Eagle House Publishing, 2004).
    To find: Search keywords Advanced Selling.

Easy Step-by-Step Guide to Telemarketing, Cold Calling and Appointment Making by Pauline Rowson (Rowmark, 2002).
    To find: Search keywords Cold Calling.

Power Sales Writing by Sue Hershkowitz-Coore (McGraw-Hill, 2003).
    To find: Search keywords Sales Writing.

NATIONAL ASSOCIATION OF REALTORS®
Real Estate Bookshelf at REALTOR.org/store

Items for sale. To find each, search by the title at REALTOR.org/store.

The Complete Idiot's Guide to Success as a Real Estate Agent by Marilyn Sullivan (Alpha, 2003) (Item #141–122).

FSBO Laptop CD Presentation by Mark Leader (Item #141–108).

FSBO Presentation Book by Mark Leader (Item #141–107).

The Lead Ladder: Painlessly Turning Strangers into Clients, One Step at a Time by Marcus Schaller (Purple Dot Group, 2005) (Item #141–164).

Marketing Library CD Collection by Pat Zaby (Item #141–195).

Mark's Money Makers by Mark Leader (Item #141–110).

2005 Profile of Referral and Relocation Activity (Item #186–28–05).

Additional Resources Available from Amazon.com or Other Online Retailers

Dare to Be There: Power Prospecting DVD by David Knox (David Knox Productions Inc., 2004).

How to Become a Power Agent in Real Estate by Darryl Davis (McGraw-Hill, 2002).

How to List and Sell Real Estate: Executing New Basics for Higher Profits by Danielle Kennedy with Warren Jamison (Thomson South-Western, 2002).

CHAPTER 2   *Selling*

Articles

"7 Steps to Preparing for an Open House" (REALTOR® Magazine Online).
    To find: Search by title at REALTOR.org/realtormag. (Requires NAR member login.)

"Menus for Real Estate Open Houses" (*Realty Times*, April 4, 2006).
    To find: Search by title at www.realtytimes.com.

"10 Tips for Selling in the Fall" (*Realty Times*, Oct. 4, 2005).
    To find: Search by title at www.realtytimes.com.

"The Basics of Representing Foreign Buyers in the U.S." (*Global Perspectives in Real Estate*, 4th Quarter 2005).
    To find: Search by title at REALTOR.org.

"Going Global" (REALTOR® Magazine Online, Sept. 2006).
    To find: Search by title at REALTOR.org/realtormag.
    Smart real estate practitioners are learning to cash in on
    global opportunities.

"How to Develop Leads for International Business" (NVAR.com
e-News Update, May 21, 2001).
    To find: Search by Developing Leads for International
    Business at www.nvar.com.

"How to Reach the Immigrant Home Buyer" (REALTOR®
Magazine Online, April 2005).
    To find: Search by title at REALTOR.org/realtormag.
    Highlights credit barriers, language proficiency, and cultural
    sensitivity.

"Meeting the Needs of the Melting Pot: Business Opportunities in
Emerging Markets" (*Real Estate Business*, April/May 2006).
    To find: Search by title at www.rebmagazine.com
    Minorities and new immigrants—traditionally underserved
    markets—will generate more than half of all first-time home
    purchases.

"A Second Home in Bulgaria" (*The New York Times*, Oct. 28, 2005).
    To find: Search by title at www.nyt.com.
    Savvy second-home buyers are snapping up homes in far-
    flung countries.

"Speaking in Tongues: Multilingual REALTORS® Find
Success with Second Language" (NVAR.com *e-News Update*,
July 10, 2001).
    To find: Search by Speaking in Tongues at www.nvar.com.

"Working with People from Southeast and Asian Cultures"
(*Wisconsin Real Estate Magazine*, April 6, 2006).
    www.news.wra.org/story.asp?a=359

"Boost Curb Appeal, Add Drama with Lighting" (REALTOR®
Magazine Online, April 13, 2006).
> To find: Search by title at REALTOR.org/realtormag.
> Four simple ideas for preparing for an open house with
> lighting.

"Feng Shui's Five Elements for Environmental Satisfaction"
(*Realty Times*, Feb. 19, 2004).
> To find: Search by title at www.realtytimes.com.

"Using Feng Shui to Help a Home Sell" (*Realty Times*, Feb. 10,
2004).
> To find: Search by title at www.realtytimes.com.

"Choices that Will Affect Your Loan" (REALTOR® Magazine
Online).
> To find: Search by title at REALTOR.org/realtormag.
> (Requires NAR member login.)
> Explains the types of loan options, including balloon and
> government-backed.

"Home Buyers Not Afraid of Risky Loans" (REALTOR® Magazine
Online, Oct. 2005).
> To find: Search by title at REALTOR.org/realtormag.
> Lists four creative mortgage options.

"Mortgage Options for Tricky Situations" (REALTOR® Magazine
Online, Feb. 20, 2006).
> To find: Search by title at REALTOR.org/realtormag.
> Covers bridge loans and 100 percent financing options.

"Which Mortgage? A Complicated Tale" (*The New York Times*,
July 17, 2005).

To find: Search by title at www.nyt.com. (There is a $3.95 charge to access some articles in the NYT Archives.)

"I'm Worth It!" (REALTOR® Magazine Online, Jan. 2003).
    To find: Search by title at REALTOR.org/realtormag.
    Ways to justify your commission.

"Overcoming Commission Objections" (REALTOR® Magazine Online, June 2003).
    To find: Search by title at REALTOR.org/realtormag. (You may need to scroll down to find link.)

"Prove You're Worth the Commission" (REALTOR® Magazine Online, Nov. 2005).
    To find: Search by title at REALTOR.org.
    Overcoming sellers' commission objections.

"Happy Returns" (REALTOR® Magazine Online, July 2005).
    To find: Search by title at REALTOR.org/realtormag.
    Closing-gift ideas.

"Five Secrets to Listing Success" (*Pennsylvania REALTOR®*, March 2006).
    To find: Search by title at www.parealtor.org.

"Too Much of a Good Thing?" (REALTOR® Magazine Online, Sept. 2004).
    To find: Search by title at REALTOR.org/realtormag, and click the link for Law: Multiple Offers (2004).
    Tips on handling multiple offers.

"Video: Listing Face-off" (REALTOR® Magazine Online, Feb. 2006).
    To find: Search by title at REALTOR.org/realtormag.
    Consumers react to three listing presentations.

NATIONAL ASSOCIATION OF REALTORS® Field Guides and REALTOR® Magazine Online Sections

Field Guide to Business Etiquette When Working with Other Cultures
    REALTOR.org/libweb.nsf/pages/fg225

Field Guide to Diversity for REALTORS®
    REALTOR.org/libweb.nsf/pages/fg215

Field Guide to Feng Shui and Vaastu
    REALTOR.org/libweb.nsf/pages/fg315

Field Guide to Getting a Mortgage
    REALTOR.org/libweb.nsf/pages/fg323

Field Guide to Home Inspections
    REALTOR.org/libweb.nsf/pages/fg311

Field Guide to Open Houses
    REALTOR.org/libweb.nsf/pages/fg207

Field Guide to REALTORS® and the Global Marketplace
    REALTOR.org/libweb.nsf/pages/fg214

Listing section
    To find: Click Listing under Selling at
    REALTOR.org/realtormag. (Requires NAR member login.)

Negotiating section
    To find: Click Negotiating under Selling at
    REALTOR.org/realtormag. (Requires NAR member login.)
    Includes resources on handling multiple offers.

Property Marketing section
> To find: Click Property Marketing under Selling at
> REALTOR.org/realtormag. (Requires NAR member login.)
> Includes resources on holding open houses.

Servicing Your Multicultural Clients section
> To find: Search by title at REALTOR.org/realtormag.
> (Requires NAR member login.)

REALTOR.org Resources

At Home With Diversity: One America
> www.realtor.org/divweb.nsf
> NAR program promotes affordable housing opportunities
for all Americans.

"Advice to Investors in Eastern Europe" (*Global Perspectives in Real Estate*, First Quarter 2003).
> To find: Search by title at REALTOR.org.

CIPS (Certified International Property Specialist) Network
> REALTOR.org/cipshome.nsf/pages/aboutcips

CIPS Network Country Profiles
> REALTOR.org/intlprof.nsf

International home page at REALTOR.org
> REALTOR.org/international

"Venturing Abroad! So You Want to Open an Office in Another Country . . ." (*Global Perspectives in Real Estate*, First Quarter 2004).
> To find: Search by title at REALTOR.org.

WorldProperties.com
> Organization helps its broker members facilitate transnational
referrals and consumers find properties outside their country.

"Presenting and Negotiating Multiple Offers: White Paper"
(NATIONAL ASSOCIATION OF REALTORS®, May 2005).
   To find: Search by Multiple Offers at REALTOR.org.
   (Requires NAR member login.)

"Shopping for a Mortgage? Do Your Homework First" (Specialty
Mortgages) (NATIONAL ASSOCIATION OF REALTORS®,
Aug. 2005).
   To find: Search by title at REALTOR.org.

"Shopping for a Mortgage? Do Your Homework First"
(Traditional Mortgages) NATIONAL ASSOCIATION OF
REALTORS®, Oct. 2005).
   To find: Search by Traditional Mortgage at REALTOR.org.
   Then click Download the brochure to launch the PDF.

NATIONAL ASSOCIATION OF REALTORS®
Virtual Library eBooks Collection

Check out books online for free at ebooks.REALTOR.org. (eBooks
are available to NAR members only. Access requires NAR member
number.)

The 10 Immutable Laws of Power Selling by James Desena (McGraw-
Hill, 2004).
   To find: Search keywords Power Selling.

*Advanced Selling Strategies: The Proven System of Sales Ideas,
Methods, and Techniques Used by Top Salespeople Everywhere* by
Brian Tracy (Eagle House Publishing, 2004).
   To find: Search keywords Advanced Selling.

Beating the Deal Killers by Stephen Giglio (McGraw-Hill, 2002).
   To find: Search keywords Deal Killers.

Connective Selling: The Secret of Winning 'Big Ticket' Sales by John Timperley (Capstone, 2004).
> To find: Search key word Connective.

Stop Telling, Start Selling: How to Use Customer-focused Dialogue to Close Sales by Linda Richardson (McGraw-Hill, 1997).
> To find: Search keywords Stop Telling.

Chinese Business Etiquette and Culture by Kevin B. Bucknall (Boson Books, 1999).
> To find: Search keywords Chinese Business.

Japan: Doing Business in a Unique Culture by Kevin B. Bucknall (Boson Books, 2006).
> To find: Search keywords Unique Culture.

The Learning Annex Presents Feng Shui by Meihwa Lin (John Wiley & Sons, 2004).
> To find: Search keywords Feng Shui.

Multicultural Manners: Essential Rules of Etiquette for the 21st Century by Norine Dresser (John Wiley & Sons, 2005).
> To find: Search keywords Multicultural Manners.

The Mortgage Answer Book: Choosing the Right Loan for You by John J. Talamo (Sourcebooks, 2005).
> To find: Search keywords Mortgage Answer.

NATIONAL ASSOCIATION OF REALTORS®
Real Estate Bookshelf at REALTOR.org/store

Items for sale. To find each, search by title at REALTOR.org/store.

At Home with Diversity, One America (course kit) (Item #190–01).

Buy Your Home Smarter with Feng Shui by Holly Ziegler (Dragon Chi, 2004) (book) (Item 141–136).
> Also available as audio CD.

Expand Your Market Training Kit (Item #126–359–04).

Insights: Focusing on the Hispanic/Latino Buyer by Marcie Roggow and Amy S. Tolbert (CD-ROM) (Item #141–191).

Feng Shui Secrets for the Real Estate Top Producer by Holly Ziegler (DVD) (Item #141–181).

North America's Greatest Commission Techniques by Mark Leader (audio CD) (Item #141–109).
> Overcoming sellers' commission objections.

Sell Your Home Faster with Feng Shui by Holly Ziegler (Dragon Chi, 2001) (book) (Item #141–120).
> Also available as audio CD.

Mortgage Education for Real Estate Professionals by Martin Koellhoffer (Mortgage Planning Solutions, 2005) (book) (Item #141–185).

Specialty Mortgages: What Are the Risks and Advantages? (brochure) (Item #126–105).
> Also available in Spanish.

Traditional Mortgages: Understanding Your Options (brochure) (Item #126–125).

Additional Resources Available from Amazon.com or Other Online Retailers

How to List and Sell Real Estate: Executing New Basics for Higher Profits by Danielle Kennedy with Warren Jamison (Thomson South-Western, 2003).

International Real Estate: A Comparative Approach by
 Mark Lee Levine (Dearborn Real Estate Education,
2004).

Investing in International Real Estate by Mary Alice Hines
(Quorum, 2000).

Japan Real Estate Investment by Mary Alice Hines
(Quorum, 2001).

Make Millions Selling Real Estate: Earning Secrets of Top Agents by
Jim Remley (AMACOM, 2005).

Mastering the Art of Selling Real Estate by Tom Hopkins
(Penguin, 2004).

CHAPTER 3   *Know Your Market*

Articles

"50 Must-have Features for Today's Home Buyers; What Baby
Boomers, Generation X, and Echo Boomers Crave for Their New
Homes" (*Professional Builder*, June 1, 2006).
    To find: Search 50 Must-have Features at www.housing
    zone.com.

"I want my MTV (and DVD and DSL)" (*Builder*, Aug. 2005).
    To find: Search by title at www.builderonline.com.
    Home technology today is about blending in with the
    lifestyles of Generation X and Generation Y.

"The New Face of Aging" (REALTOR® Magazine Online, March
2006).
    To find: Search by title at REALTOR.org/realtormag.

"The New Mudroom: Matching Lifestyles with Innovation"
(*Realty Times*, Feb. 9, 2006).
>   To find: Search by title at www.realtytimes.com.

"Bypass Competitors: Find a Niche" (REALTOR® Magazine
Online, Aug. 2002).
>   To find: Search Bypass the Competition at
>   REALTOR.org/realtormag.

"Finding Your Niche" (REALTOR® Magazine Online).
>   To find: Search by title at REALTOR.org/realtormag.
>   (Requires NAR member login.)

"How I Found My Niche" (REALTOR® Magazine Online,
April 2004).
>   To find: Search by title at REALTOR.org/realtormag.

"A Rare Niche: New Homes for Rent" (*The New York Times*,
Sept. 4, 2005).
>   To find: Search by title at www.nyt.com. There may be a
> $3.95 charge to access some articles in the NYT Archives.

"Real Estate Agents Reach out to Gay Home Buyers"
(*Milwaukee Journal Sentinel*, Sept. 5, 2005).
>   To find: Search by title at www.jsonline.com.

NATIONAL ASSOCIATION OF REALTORS® Field Guides

Field Guide to Listing and Selling Luxury Properties
>   REALTOR.org/libweb.nsf/pages/fg306

Field Guide to Marketing to the 55+ Population
>   REALTOR.org/libweb.nsf/pages/fg211

Field Guide to Marketing to the Hispanic Community
>   REALTOR.org/libweb.nsf/pages/fg221

Field Guide to Working with Empowered Consumers
REALTOR.org/libweb.nsf/pages/fg213

NATIONAL ASSOCIATION OF REALTORS®
Virtual Library eBooks Collection

Check out books online for free at ebooks.REALTOR.org. (eBooks are available to NAR members only. Access requires NAR member number.)

Buying a Home When You're Single by Donna G. Albrecht (John Wiley & Sons, 2001).
    To find: Search keywords You're Single.

Cities Ranked & Rated: More than 400 Metropolitan Areas Evaluated in the U.S. and Canada by Bert Sperling and Peter Sander (John Wiley & Sons, 2004).
    To find: Search keywords Cities Ranked.

Community by Design: New Urbanism for Suburbs and Small Communities by Kenneth Hall and Gerald Porterfield (McGraw-Hill, 2001).
    To find: Search keywords By Design.

NATIONAL ASSOCIATION OF REALTORS®
Real Estate Bookshelf at REALTOR.org/store

Items for sale. To find each, search by title at REALTOR.org/store.

Cashing in on a Second Home in Mexico by Tom Kelly and Mitch Creekmore (Crabman, 2005) (Item #141–173).

2006 NAR Baby Boomers and Real Estate: Today and Tomorrow (Item #186–77–06).

Additional Resources Available from Amazon.com or Other Online Retailers

Reaching Out: The Financial Power of Niche Marketing by Doris Barrell and Mark Nash (Dearborn Real Estate Education, 2003).

Targeting the Over 55 Client by Buddy West and Betsy West (Dearborn Real Estate Education, 1998).

CHAPTER 4 *Stay Out of Trouble*

Articles

"Buying? Twelve Red Flags That Should Raise Concern" (*Realty Times*, Nov. 11, 2003).
   To find: Search by Twelve Red Flags at www.realtytimes.com.
   Home defects to be on the lookout for.

"Spot Landscaping Red Flags" (REALTOR® Magazine Online, Aug. 2005).
   To find: Search by title at REALTOR.org/realtormag. (You may need to scroll down to find link.)

"Educate Yourself on Mortgage Fraud" (REALTOR® Magazine Online, Nov. 2005).
   To find: Search by title at REALTOR.org.

"Ten Warning Signs of Predatory Lending" (Mortgage Bankers Association, 2002).
   www.stopmortgagefraud.com/signs.htm.

"Save Yourself from a Lawsuit: Document, Document, Document" (*Realty Times*, Feb. 20, 2004).
   To find: Search by Save Yourself from a Lawsuit at www.realtytimes.com.

"Be Safe at Listings" (*Ohio REALTOR®*, June 2003).
    To find: Search by title at www.ohiorealtors.org.

"Ten Safety Tips for Meeting Prospective Clients"
(*Pennsylvania REALTOR®*, Sept. 2005).
    To find: Search by Ten Safety Tips at www.parealtor.org.

"To Meet or Not to Meet?" (REALTOR® Magazine Online,
Sept. 2003).
    To find: Search by title at REALTOR.org/realtormag.
    (You may need to scroll down to the link.)
    Safety reasons for encouraging prospects to meet you at your
office.

NATIONAL ASSOCIATION OF REALTORS® Field Guides and REALTOR® Magazine Online Sections

Field Guide to 1031 Exchanges
    REALTOR.org/libweb.nsf/pages/fg408

Field Guide to Do-Not-Call, Do-Not-Fax, and Do-Not-E-Mail
Laws
    REALTOR.org/libweb.nsf/pages/fg707

Field Guide to Fair Housing
    REALTOR.org/libweb.nsf/pages/fg705

Field Guide to Identity Theft
    REALTOR.org/libweb.nsf/pages/fg909

Field Guide to Mortgage Fraud
    REALTOR.org/libweb.nsf/pages/fg330

Field Guide to REALTOR® Safety
    REALTOR.org/libweb.nsf/pages/fg201

Property Marketing section
>   To find: Click Property Marketing under Selling at
>   REALTOR.org/realtormag. (Requires NAR member login.)
>   For fair housing and property disclosure articles.

Risk Management section
>   To find: Click Risk Management under Brokerage
>   Management at REALTOR.org/realtormag. (Requires
>   NAR member login.)

Sales Meeting section
>   To find: Click Prepackaged Sales Meetings under Brokerage
>   Management at REALTOR.org/realtormag. (Requires
>   NAR member login.)

REALTOR.org Resources

Frequently Asked RESPA Questions
>   To find: Search by title at REALTOR.org. (Requires
>   NAR member login.)

REALTOR® Safety Week
>   REALTOR.org/safety

NATIONAL ASSOCIATION OF REALTORS®
Virtual Library eBooks Collection

Check out books online for free at ebooks.REALTOR.org. (eBooks
are available to NAR members only. Access requires NAR member
number.)

Be Alert, Be Aware, Have a Plan by Neal Rawls with Susan Kovach
(The Globe Pequot Press, 2002).
>   To find: Search keywords Be Alert.

The Complete Book of Home Inspection by Norman Becker (McGraw-Hill, 2002).

   To find: Search keywords Home Inspection.

The Tax-Free Exchange Loophole by Jack Cummings (John Wiley & Sons, 2005).

   To find: Search keywords Tax-Free.

NATIONAL ASSOCIATION OF REALTORS®
Real Estate Bookshelf at REALTOR.org/store

Items for sale. Unless otherwise indicated, to find each, search by title at REALTOR.org/store.

Don't Be a Victim: Personal Safety for REALTORS® (video) (Item #V150–25).

   To find: Search by Don't Be a Victim at REALTOR.org/store.

The Facts About Mold (Item #141–30).

A Guide to Mold, Moisture and Your Home (Item #141–24).

Independent Contractors in Real Estate, a Guide for Risk Management (Item #126–371).

   To find: Search by Independent Contractors at REALTOR.org/store.

Lead-based Paint Reference Guide (Item #141–558).

Property Disclosures Pocket Guide (Item #126–343).

Protect Your Family from Lead in Your Home (Item #141–40).

   To find: Search by Protect Your Family from Lead at REALTOR.org/store.

Real Estate Brokerage Essentials: Managing Business and Legal Issues (Item # 126–358).

   To find: Search by Real Estate Brokerage Essentials at REALTOR.org/store.

REALTOR® Safety Tips Card (Item #150–50).
    To find: Search by Safety Tips at REALTOR.org/store.

Sexual Harassment: Awareness and Prevention Pocket Guide
(Item #126–149).
    To find: Search by Sexual Harassment: Awareness at
    REALTOR.org/store.

Sexual Harassment Video (Item #126–150V).

Workplace Law and Office Policies, a Guide for Risk Management
(Item #126–373).
    To find: Search by Workplace Law and Office Policies at
    REALTOR.org/store.

Additional Resources Available from Amazon.com or Other Online Retailers

The Digital Paper Trail in Real Estate Transactions by Oliver E.
Frascona and Katherine E. Reece (Real Law Books, 2003).

*The Real Estate Agent's Field Guide: Essential Insider Advice for
Surviving in a Competitive Market* by Bridget McCrea
(AMACOM, 2004).

Red Flags: Property Inspection Guide by James C. Prendergast and
Lynn P. Cushwa (Dearborn Real Estate Education, 2005).

Risk Hotline for Real Estate by Robert L. Read (Classic Day
Publishing, 2005).

Other Resources

Environmental Protection Agency
    www.epa.gov

National Lead Information Center
   www.epa.gov/lead/pubs/nlic.htm

U.S. Department of Housing and Urban Development
(Fair Housing and RESPA information)
   www.hud.gov

CHAPTER 5   *Personal Growth*

Articles

"8 Ways to Balance Your Work and Family Life" (REALTOR®
Magazine Online, May 2005).
   To find: Search by title at REALTOR.org/realtormag.

"Curbing Burnout in the 24/7 Salesperson" (REALTOR®
Magazine Online, July 2000).
   To find: Search by title at REALTOR.org/realtormag.

"Feeling Stressed Out? Take Action Now to Avert Career
Burnout" (*Austin Business Journal*, June 17, 2005).
   To Find: Click Search Archive at
   www.bizjournals.com/austin. Then search by keywords Career
   Burnout and choose 2005 from the Date Menu.

"Life-Work Balance Equals Success" (REALTOR® Magazine
Online, May 2002).
   To find: Search by title at REALTOR.org.

NATIONAL ASSOCIATION OF REALTORS® Field Guides and REALTOR® Magazine Online Sections

Field Guide to Balancing Work and Family Life
   REALTOR.org/libweb.nsf/pages/fg119

Field Guide to Career Advice for REALTORS®
    REALTOR.org/libweb.nsf/pages/fg116
    Includes section on avoiding burnout.

Becoming a Volunteer and Leading a Charity sections
    To find: Click Good Neighbor Awards logo on home page at
    REALTOR.org/realtormag and then either Becoming a
    Volunteer or Leading a Charity under Good Neighbor Tool Kit.

NATIONAL ASSOCIATION OF REALTORS®
Virtual Library eBooks Collection

Check out books online for free at ebooks.REALTOR.org. (eBooks
are available to NAR members only. Access requires NAR member
number.)

The 10-Minute Stress Manager by Emmett Miller (Hay House, 2005).
    To find: Search keywords Stress Manager.

E-mail Etiquette by Samantha Miller (Warner Books, 2001).
    To find: Search keywords E-mail Etiquette.

Find the Balance by Deborah Tom (BBC Audiobooks, 2006).
    To find: Search keywords Find the Balance.

Get a Grip! Overcoming Stress and Thriving in the Workplace by Bob
Losyk (John Wiley & Sons, 2004).
    To find: Search keywords Get a Grip.

Harvard Business Review on Work and Life Balance (Harvard
Business School Press, 2000).
    To find: Search keywords Life Balance.

Improve Your Memory by Gary Small (Sounds True, 2003).
    To find: Search by title.

Learn to Relax by C. Eugene Walker and Shauna Zurbrugg
(Penton Overseas, 2001).
    To find: Search by title.

Stress Management Sourcebook by J. Barton Cunningham
(McGraw-Hill, 2000).
    To find: Search by title.

NATIONAL ASSOCIATION OF REALTORS®
Real Estate Bookshelf at REALTOR.org/store

Items for sale.

FamilyTime DVD (Item #FAM).
    To find: Search by title at REALTOR.org/store.

Says Who? by Johnnie Johnson (Growing Tree Learning Center,
2006) (Item #141–162).
    To find: Search by Says Who at REALTOR.org/store.
    Success strategies and critical thinking skills for staying
    focused on goals.

Additional Resources Available from Amazon.com or
Other Online Retailers

Beat Sales Burnout by Stephan Schiffman (Adams Media
Corporation, 2005).

Dress Your Best by Stacy London and Clinton Kelly (Three Rivers
Press, 2005).

WorkingMoms.Calm: How Smart Women Balance Family & Career by
Danielle Kennedy (Thomson South-Western, 2002).

CHAPTER 6   *Professional Development*

Articles

"90 Days to Real Estate Success: A Week-by-Week Guide"
(REALTOR® Magazine Online, Feb. 2005).
　　To find: Search by title at REALTOR.org/realtormag.

"Find Mentors: Follow that Leader" (REALTOR® Magazine
Online, Feb. 2002).
　　To find: Search by title at REALTOR.org/realtormag.

"It's Not Easy Being Green" (REALTOR® Magazine Online,
Aug. 2004).
　　To find: Search by title at REALTOR.org/realtormag.

"Learning from the Pros" (*Commercial Investment Real Estate
Magazine*, Sept./Oct. 2005).
　　To find: Search by title at www.ciremagazine.com.

"Take the High Road" (REALTOR® Magazine Online,
May 2005).
　　To find: Search by title at REALTOR.org/realtormag.
　　How to be ethical every day.

"Strategic Networking Tips: There's a Skill to Meeting People"
(WomensMedia.com).
　　To find: Search by Strategic Networking Tips at
　　www.womensmedia.com.

"When You're on Stage . . . You're Selling" (REALTOR® Magazine
Online, Feb. 2002).
　　To find: Search by title at REALTOR.org/realtormag.

NATIONAL ASSOCIATION OF REALTORS® Field Guides and REALTOR® Magazine Online Sections

Field Guide to Mentoring
    REALTOR.org/libweb.nsf/pages/fg108

Field Guide to Professional Standards
    REALTOR.org/libweb.nsf/pages/fg600

Field Guide to Quick Real Estate Statistics
    REALTOR.org/libweb.nsf/pages/fg006

Field Guide to Tips for New REALTORS®
    REALTOR.org/libweb.nsf/pages/fg200

For Rookies section
    To find: Click For Rookies under Selling at
    REALTOR.org/realtormag.

REALTOR.org Resources

Code of Ethics and Standards of Practice
    To find: Search by title at REALTOR.org.

Code of Ethics and Arbitration Manual
    To find: Search by title at REALTOR.org. (Requires NAR
    member login.)

Careers in Real Estate
    To find: Search by title at REALTOR.org.

NATIONAL ASSOCIATION OF REALTORS®
Virtual Library eBooks Collection

Check out books online for free at ebooks.REALTOR.org. (eBooks
are available to NAR members only. Access requires NAR member
number.)

7 Steps to Fearless Speaking by Lilyan Wilder (Penton Overseas, 1999).
    To find: Search keywords Fearless Speaking.

Careers in Real Estate by Mark Rowh (McGraw-Hill, 2002).
    To find: Search by title.

The Complete Guide to Public Speaking by Jeff Davidson (John Wiley & Sons, 2001).
    To find: Search by title.

Maverick Real Estate Investing: The Art of Buying and Selling Properties like Trump, Zell, Simon, and the World's Greatest Land Owners by Steve Bergsman (John Wiley & Sons, 2005).
    To find: Search keywords Maverick Real Estate Investing.

Mentored by a Millionaire: Master Strategies of Super Achievers by Steven K. Scott (John Wiley & Sons, 2004).
    To find: Search keywords Mentored by a Millionaire.

The Networking Survival Guide by Diane Darling (McGraw-Hill, 2003).
    To find: Search keywords Networking Survival.

Opportunities in Real Estate Careers by Mariwyn Evans (McGraw-Hill, 1997).
    To find: Search by title.

Power Mentoring by Ellen Ensher and Susan Murphy (John Wiley & Sons, 2005).
    To find: Search by title.

Public Speaking by Jacey Lamerton (HarperCollins, 2001).
    To find: Search by title.

Speak with Confidence by Dianna Booher (McGraw-Hill, 2002).
    To find: Search by title.

NATIONAL ASSOCIATION OF REALTORS®
Real Estate Bookshelf at REALTOR.org/store

Items for sale. Unless otherwise indicated, to find each, search by title at REALTOR.org/store.

Code of Ethics and Standards of Practice Pamphlet
(Item #166–288).

FamilyTime DVD (Item #FAM).

The PMZ Way: Strategies of Highly Successful Real Estate Agents by Michael P. Zagaris (PMZ Publishing, 2005) (Item #141–150).
   To find: Search by The PMZ Way.

Professionalism in Real Estate Practice (booklet) (Item #166–1113).

Red Hot Rookie by Mark Leader (audio CD and manual)
(Item #141–105).

For the latest version of NAR research, such as the "Member Profile" and the "Profile of Home Buyers and Sellers," search the REALTOR.org/Store.

Additional Resources Available through Amazon.com or Other Online Retailers

The Heart of Mentoring by Robert Tamasy and David A. Stoddard (Navpress Publishing, 2003).

The Millionaire Maker: Act, Think, and Make Money the Way the Wealthy Do by Loral Langemeier (McGraw-Hill, 2005).

The Millionaire Real Estate Agent by Gary Keller (McGraw-Hill, 2004).

Up and Running in 30 Days by Carla Cross (Dearborn Real Estate Education, 2001).

Voice Power: Using Your Voice to Captivate, Persuade, and Command Attention by Renee Grant-Williams (AMACOM, 2002).

Your 1st Year in Real Estate by Dirk Zeller (Prima Publishers, 2001).

CHAPTER 7   *Time Management*

Articles

"Assistant Insights" (REALTOR® Magazine Online, Feb. 2002).
   To find: Search by Personal Assistant Insights at
   REALTOR.org/realtormag.

"Make More Money with the 80/20 Principle" (REALTOR®
Magazine Online, April 2005).
   To find: Search by title at REALTOR.org/realtormag.

"Schedule Your Way to Productivity" (REALTOR® Magazine
Online, April 2003).
   To find: Search by title at REALTOR.org/realtormag.

"Ten Time Savers" (*Realty Times*, Jan. 24, 2006).
   To find: Search by title at www.realtytimes.com.

"The Top Five Time Management Mistakes" (*Realty Times*, Sept.
20, 2006).
   To find: Search by title at www.realtytimes.com.

"Have a Successful Career and Still Have a Life" (REALTOR®
Magazine Online, June 2005).
   To find: Search by title at REALTOR.org.

"Work? Give It a Rest. With Planning, You Can Limit How Much
the Office Encroaches on Your Vacation" (*The Charlotte Observer*,
April 30, 2006).
   To find: From the *Charlotte Observer* search box (choose
   Archives) at www.charlotte.com, search keywords Office

Encroaches. (Requires web site registration. There's a $2.95 charge for single articles).

"Breakdown: What to Keep in Your Car in Case of Emergency" (*Road & Travel Magazine*).
> To find: Search by title at www.roadandtravel.com.

NATIONAL ASSOCIATION OF REALTORS® Field Guides and REALTOR® Magazine Online Sections

Field Guide to Organizing Your Office
> REALTOR.org/libweb.nsf/pages/fg120

Field Guide to Personal Assistants
> REALTOR.org/libweb.nsf/pages/fg114

Field Guide to Productivity for REALTORS®
> REALTOR.org/libweb.nsf/pages/fg217

Field Guide to Time Management for Real Estate Professionals
> REALTOR.org/libweb.nsf/pages/fg208

Better Time Management sales meeting (NAR member login required.)
> To access: Click Prepackaged Sales Meetings under Brokerage Management at REALTOR.org/realtormag. Then click Better Time Management.

Personal Assistants section (NAR member login required.)
> To find: Click Personal Assistants under Selling at REALTOR.org/realtormag.

REALTOR.org Resource

Real Estate Professional Assistant certificate course
> www.professional-assistant.com

NATIONAL ASSOCIATION OF REALTORS®
Virtual Library eBooks Collection

Check out books online for free at ebooks.REALTOR.org. (eBooks are available to NAR members only. Access requires NAR member number.)

Easy Step-by-Step Guide to Stress and Time Management by Brian Lomas (Rowmark, 2000).
    To find: Search keywords Stress and Time Management.

E-mail Etiquette by Samantha Miller (Warner Books, 2001).
    To find: Search by title.
    Includes section on e-mail overload.

The Learning Annex Presents Uncluttering Your Space by Ann T. Sullivan (John Wiley & Sons, 2004).
    To find: Search keyword Uncluttering.

Manage Your Time and Double Your Productivity by Brian Tracy (Eagle House Publishing, 2004).
    To find: Search by title.

Time Management by Marc Mancini (McGraw-Hill, 2003).
    To find: Search by title.

NATIONAL ASSOCIATION OF REALTORS®
Real Estate Bookshelf at REALTOR.org/store

Items for sale.

Playing with the BIG BOYS & GIRLS in Real Estate (audio CD set) (Item #141–153).
    To find: Search by Playing with the Big Boys & Girls at REALTOR.org/store.
    Contains section on the principles of time management. Also available as a book.

Real Estate Assistants, A Guide for Risk Management
(Item #126–370).

To find: Search by title at REALTOR.org/store.

Additional Resources Available through Amazon.com or Other Online Retailers

Clutter-Proof Your Business: Turn Your Mess into Success by Mike Nelson (Career Press, 2002).

Conquering Chaos at Work by Harriet Schechter (Fireside, 2000).

The Home Office Solution: How to Balance Your Professional and Personal Lives While Working at Home by Alice Bredin (John Wiley & Sons, 1998).

Organizing for Dummies by Eileen Roth and Elizabeth Miles (Hungry Minds, 2000).

Organizing for Success by Kenneth Zeigler (McGraw-Hill, 2005).

Organizing Your Home Office for Success: Expert Strategies that can Work for You by Lisa Kanarek (Blakely Press, 1998).

Organize Your Office! Simple Routines for Managing Your Workspace by Ronni Eisenberg (Hyperion, 1999).

Organizing Your Work Space: A Guide to Personal Productivity by Odette Pollar (Crisp Learning, 1999).

Taming the Paper Tiger at Work by Barbara Hemphill (Kaplan Business, 1998).

Note: URLs for additional resources are subject to change.

About the NATIONAL ASSOCIATION OF REALTORS®

The NATIONAL ASSOCIATION OF REALTORS®, "The Voice for Real Estate," is the largest professional trade association in the United States, representing more than 1.3 million members. NAR's members include residential and commercial brokers, salespeople, property managers, appraisers, counselors, and others engaged in all aspects of real estate. Members belong to one or more of some 1,400 local associations and boards and 54 state and territory associations. They're pledged to a strict Code of Ethics and standards of practice.

Working for America's property owners, NAR strives to be the leading advocate in the United States of the right to own, use, and transfer real property and is the acknowledged leader in developing standards for efficient, effective, and ethical real estate business practices. The association provides a facility for professional development, research, and exchange of information among its members, the public, and the government for the purpose of preserving the free enterprise system and the right to own real property.

The term REALTOR® is a registered collective membership mark that identifies a real estate professional who is a member of NAR and subscribes to its strict Code of Ethics.

More Online: Read about NAR's mission, organization, and history under "About NAR" on the homepage at REALTOR.org.

About the REALTOR® Code of Ethics

The term REALTOR® has come to connote competency, fairness, and high integrity resulting from adherence to a lofty ideal of moral conduct in business relations. No inducement of profit and no instruction from clients ever can justify departure from this ideal.

> *—From the Preamble of the Code of Ethics and
> Standards of Practice of the NATIONAL
> ASSOCIATION OF REALTORS®*

The REALTOR® Code of Ethics is a hallmark in efforts by the NATIONAL ASSOCIATION OF REALTORS® to help maintain the professional success of its members. To keep their good standing in the association, REALTORS® complete training in the Code of Ethics every four years and are subject to disciplinary action for failure to complete the training or for conduct that's not in accordance with the Code, which is updated regularly by the association's Board of Directors.

The Code of Ethics is organized into 17 articles and dozens of Standards of Practice through which are enumerated the duties of REALTORS® to their clients and customers, the public, and other REALTORS®. The preamble is reproduced here, and the Code, in its entirety, is published annually in the January issue of REALTOR® Magazine and maintained online at REALTOR.org in the resource portion of "About NAR."

Preamble of the Code of Ethics and Standards of Practice of the NATIONAL ASSOCIATION OF REALTORS®

Under all is the land. Upon its wise utilization and widely allocated ownership depend the survival and growth of free institutions and of our civilization. REALTORS® should recognize that the interests of the nation and its citizens require the highest and best use of the land and the widest distribution of land ownership. They require the creation of adequate housing, the building of functioning cities, the development of productive industries and farms, and the preservation of a healthful environment.

Such interests impose obligations beyond those of ordinary commerce. They impose grave social responsibility and a patriotic duty to which REALTORS® should dedicate themselves, and for which they should be diligent in preparing themselves. REALTORS®, therefore, are zealous to maintain and improve the standards of their calling and share with their fellow REALTORS® a common responsibility for its integrity and honor.

In recognition and appreciation of their obligations to clients, customers, the public, and each other, REALTORS® continuously strive to become and remain informed on issues affecting real estate and, as knowledgeable professionals, they willingly share the fruit of their experience and study with others. They identify and take steps, through enforcement of this Code of Ethics and by assisting appropriate regulatory bodies, to eliminate practices which may damage the public or which might discredit or bring dishonor to the real estate profession. REALTORS® having direct personal knowledge of conduct that may violate the Code of Ethics involving misappropriation of client or customer funds or property, willful discrimination, or fraud resulting in substantial economic harm, bring such matters to the attention of the appropriate Board or Association of REALTORS®.

Realizing that cooperation with other real estate professionals promotes the best interests of those who utilize their services, REALTORS® urge exclusive representation of clients; do not attempt to gain any unfair advantage over their competitors; and refrain from making unsolicited comments about other practitioners. In instances where their opinion is sought, or where REALTORS®

believe that comment is necessary, their opinion is offered in an objective, professional manner, uninfluenced by any personal motivation or potential advantage or gain.

The term REALTOR® has come to connote competency, fairness, and high integrity resulting from adherence to a lofty ideal of moral conduct in business relations. No inducement of profit and no instruction from clients ever can justify departure from this ideal.

In the interpretation of this obligation, REALTORS® can take no safer guide than that which has been handed down through the centuries, embodied in the Golden Rule, "Whatsoever ye would that others should do to you, do ye even so to them."

Accepting this standard as their own, REALTORS® pledge to observe its spirit in all of their activities and to conduct their business in accordance with the tenets set forth in the Code.

Index